Josh Cohen is Senior Lecturer in English and Comparative Literature at Goldsmiths University of London and the author of *Spectacular Allegories* and *Interrupting Auschwitz*.

HOW TO READ

Available now

How to Read Darwin by Mark Ridley
How to Read Freud by Josh Cohen
How to Read Hitler by Neil Gregor
How to Read Nietzsche by Keith Ansell Pearson
How to Read Sade by John Phillips
How to Read Wittgenstein by Ray Monk

Published Autumn 2005

How to Read Foucault by Ian Hacking
How to Read Heidegger by Mark Wrathall
How to Read Jung by Andrew Samuels
How to Read Marx by Peter Osborne
How to Read Shakespeare by Nicholas Royle

Forthcoming

How to Read de Beauvoir by Stella Sandford
How to Read Derrida by Penelope Deutscher
How to Read Sartre by Robert Bernasconi

FREUD

JOSH COHEN

Granta Books
London

Granta Publications, 2/3 Hanover Yard, Noel Road, London N1 8BE

First published in Great Britain by Granta Books 2005

A CIP catalogue record for this book
is available from the British Library.

1 3 5 7 9 10 8 6 4 2

Typeset by M Rules

Printed and bound in Great Britain by
Bookmarque Limited, Croydon, Surrey

CONTENTS

ACKNOWLEDGEMENTS

Special thanks to Simon Critchley for the opportunity to write this book, and to my very incisive and efficient editors, George Miller and Bella Shand. Thanks to various readers of the work in progress, especially: Philip McGowan for his unstinting eye for detail, Amy Gadney for her insight and enthusiasm, Nigel Tubbs for invaluable last-minute encouragement, and to Adrian Townsend for inspiration on slips. Thanks too to Alex Gordon for two generous and eerily appropriate gifts. And to Gregorio Kohon for help both direct and intangible.

For Abigail Cohen, my most patient, dedicated and passionately interested reader, no thanks are enough. Nor for Ethan and Reuben Cohen, whose unrelenting disruptiveness and total indifference brought Freud to life more vibrantly than any book. This one is for Reuben, in spite or because of his being the last person to need it, for now at least.

Tell X that speech is not dirty silence
Clarified. It is silence made still dirtier.

Wallace Stevens, 'The Creations of Sound'

That's how we know we're alive. We're wrong.

Philip Roth, *American Pastoral*

SERIES EDITOR'S FOREWORD

How am I to read *How to Read*?

This series is based on a very simple, but novel idea. Most beginners' guides to great thinkers and writers offer either potted biography or condensed summaries of their major works, or perhaps even both. *How to Read*, by contrast, brings the reader face-to-face with the writing itself in the company of an expert guide. Its starting point is that in order to get close to what a writer is all about, you have to get close to the words they actually use and be shown how to read those words.

Every book in the series is in a way a masterclass in reading. Each author has selected ten or so short extracts from a writer's work and looks at them in detail as a way of revealing their central ideas and thereby opening doors onto a whole world of thought. Sometimes these extracts are arranged chronologically to give a sense of a thinker's development over time, sometimes not. The books are not merely compilations of a thinker's most famous passages, their 'greatest hits', but rather they offer a series of clues or keys that will enable readers to go on and make discoveries of their own. In addition to the texts and readings, each book provides a short biographical chronology and suggestions for further reading, internet resources, and so on. The books in the *How to Read* series don't claim to tell you all you need to know about Freud, Nietzsche and Darwin, or indeed Shakespeare and the Marquis de Sade, but they do offer the best starting point for further exploration.

Unlike the available second-hand of the minds that have shaped our intellectual, cultural, religious, political and scientific landscape, *How to Read* offers a refreshing set of first-hand encounters with those minds. Our hope is that these books will, by turns, instruct, intrigue, embolden, encourage and delight.

Simon Critchley
New School for Social Research, New York

Introduction

I have written this book under the stern gaze of Sigmund Freud.

Sitting on the shelf just above me, still in its original packaging, is a gift from a friend: the Sigmund Freud Action Figure. A plastic four-inch Freud with mobile arms and neck stares out imperturbably from behind his cellophane packaging. Unfortunately, neither the gravity of the unsmiling features, nor the meticulousness of the grey three-piece suit can redeem the indignity of having become a bit of novelty merchandising. Cod-Freudian phrases such as, 'Tell me about your mother' are spread across the Action Figure's box, making explicit the message already implicit in the figure itself: the man and his thoughts are now our harmlessly familiar friends, just another motif in our cultural wallpaper.

What tribute could be more ambiguous, more simultaneously elevating and belittling? Freud is now both big and small enough to be a mass-produced plastic miniature, with the brand-recognition of an Action Man. Freud lives eternally, but in the dead cells of non-biodegradable plastic. Whatever was alive in his ideas has been devitalized by mass diffusion: the once unpalatable revelations of the Oedipus complex are reduced to the comic cliché, 'Tell me about your mother'.

This is the inverse of the problem Freud had to contend with when he began to disseminate his theories. His first expositions of the buried impulses and desires that condition human life provoked in his readers and audiences many different forms of hostility: shock, disgust, wilful distortion, scientific 'refutation', ridicule. Now, by contrast, Freud's ideas have seeped so pervasively into our daily idiom that we no longer acknowledge their origin. We speak casually of one person's 'mother fixation', describe another as 'repressed', distinguish between our conscious and unconscious motivations, and, in the most dubious bit of pop-Freudianism, find sexual symbolism everywhere. None of this, of course, need indicate real knowledge of, let alone adherence to his basic premises. The assimilation of his vocabulary of the inner life coexists happily with the widespread sense that we've done, and are done with Freud. After all, hasn't he been discredited by biologists, neurologists, psychologists, anthropologists and philosophers? Didn't he think everything's about sex? Aren't his theories irredeemably sexist (or 'phallocentric'), not to mention heterosexist?

The Action Figure is an exemplary compromise, in precisely Freud's sense, between these contradictory stances of acceptance and rejection, a way of simultaneously knowing and not knowing what he has to tell us. It is also, lest we lose sight of it, a very funny comment on this compromised relationship with Freud. Reactions such as, 'Of course we believe in Freud!' and 'Of course I harbour incestuous desires (What's the big deal?)' sit alongside, 'Of course it's all nonsense!' and 'My *mother*? Are you sick? Perhaps you need help . . .'.

Action Freud, in short, points up the difficulties confronting anyone attempting an exposition of his ideas. We have to contend less with the hostility aroused by the new, than with the fatigue induced by the familiar. Freud's problem was that his startling innovations – the unconscious, repression, the Oedipus complex, the death-drive – were too alien or, to borrow Freud's term, too 'uncanny' (see Chapter Six) for his audience to absorb. The problem for us, a century later, is that they are no longer uncanny enough: we've managed to shrink them to the proportions of a plastic miniature.

My aim in this book is, above all, to restore to Freud something of his power of provocation. Freud, it bears recalling, bequeathed a body of ideas that irreversibly transformed our understanding of the world and of ourselves. All the ways in which our culture plays out its tellingly ambivalent relationship to him – the facile knowingness, the polemical attacks and defences, the popular reductions and distortions – are ultimately ways of evading the transformative power of his thought.

This is emphatically not to say that an authentic encounter with Freud should result in acceptance of what he says (as if it were in any case a straightforward question of acceptance or rejection): on the contrary, if one reads Freud without resisting him, one hasn't really read him. No one, however, can come out of an encounter with Freud with all their prejudices intact: at very least, something of one's self-image, of one's sense of what it means to be human will be unsettled. Meanwhile, for those of us who take Freud's ideas more deeply to heart, it's hard to experience anything – a novel, an advert, a glance, a conversation, a casual thought or feeling – in the same way again.

As even a glance at the chronology of his life will show, Freud's great clinical and theoretical discoveries came to him neither spontaneously nor fully formed. His biography doesn't allow us to draw a retrospective straight line from childhood to the birth of psychoanalysis. Excelling in all subjects throughout his school years, he entered Vienna

University with little inclination for the medical path he eventually chose. Nor was this choice governed by a particular ambition in the field of psychiatry. On the contrary, by the time Freud had opened his private practice for the treatment of nervous diseases in 1886 (the same practice he would retain until his departure for London in 1938), he had taken many scientific detours. An initial predilection for biology had led him to work and publish for six years on the anatomy of eels and lampreys under the tutelage of Ernst Brücke, director of the Viennese Physiological Laboratory.

Only with the prospect of marriage and the need for a larger and more secure income, did Freud divert his scholarly energies towards obtaining a medical degree, and even here his path to psychopathology was a faltering one. After graduation he continued to develop his expertise in neuroanatomy, as well as conducting pioneering experiments in the clinical use of cocaine. It was not until his 1885 visit to Paris to study at the famous Salpêtrière psychiatric hospital under the great neuropathologist Jean-Martin Charcot, that Freud's interest turned sharply towards the psychology of the neuroses. Charcot's radically new conception of hysterical symptoms as 'ideogenic' – rooted in the buried *ideas*, rather than the physiological condition, of the patient – was the first spur to his development of a new theory of, and therapy for neurosis.

Developed initially in parallel with his neuroanatomical work, Freud's new interests came in time to be his exclusive ones. In particular, his work on the aetiology (the complex of causes) and therapy of hysteria was furthered through collaboration with Josef Breuer, a senior Viennese physician. Breuer had informed him in 1882 of a young female hysteric whose treatment had led to his development of a new therapeutic technique.

'Anna O.' was relieved by Breuer of her physiological symptoms (disturbances of vision, temporary paralyses, vomiting and hallucinations) by being made to recall the 'pathogenic' or psychically toxic memories which underlay them. This method of *catharsis*, or in Anna O.'s own famous coinage, 'talking cure', became the basis of a period of intense clinical and theoretical collaboration with Freud, culminating in their joint publication in1895 of *Studies on Hysteria*, a series of five case histories (all but Anna O. were Freud's patients), as well as theoretical and technical elaborations of hysteria and its treatment.

Freud's collaboration with Breuer was the public counter-part to the more private and speculative enterprise of developing a new theory of the mind. The channel for this enterprise was his correspondence with his friend Wilhelm Fliess, a Berlin ear, nose and throat specialist and biologist (a field in which he propounded some now notoriously eccentric theses). Fliess served as effective midwife to the labour that eventually gave birth to psychoanalysis.

The Fliess correspondence vividly attests to the tortuous and protracted course of this labour. In his letters, Freud persistently develops, revises and revokes his emerging theses, most notably that of the aetiology of the neuroses. In the first part of the correspondence, as well as in his publications of this period, he identifies the causes of hysteria in actual events in the patient's past, and specifically in a traumatic childhood seduction by an older child or adult in the patient's family, a thesis that earned widespread scepticism and some disgust amongst his colleagues. In 1897, however, he came gradually to renounce this thesis as both implausible and insufficient, writing to Fliess in September that, 'I no longer believe in my *neurotica* [theory of the neuroses]'[1]. The alternative he proposed, however, was no less scandalous: neuroses were rooted in infantile phantasies[2], imaginary scenes that staged the child's transgressive wishes and retained their force into adulthood as the unconscious sources of her symptoms. Given that these phantasies, and the mechanisms by which they operate, would become the primary objects of psychoanalytic inquiry, I'll have a great deal more to say about them in the chapters that follow.

Freud offered his first systematic elaboration of the theory of unconscious phantasy in *The Interpretation of Dreams* (1900), the foundational text of psychoanalysis. The emergence of a psychoanalytic movement, however, was some way off. Widely ignored by his peers, *The Interpretation of Dreams* sold 351 copies in the first 6 years of its publication. This neglect was effectively the first chapter in a long history of resistance to psychoanalysis that has persisted to this day in multiple and changing forms.

Nevertheless, within less than a decade of the book's publication, a psychoanalytic movement had emerged, one that makes the implicit claim of authority in this book's title seem peculiarly foolhardy. Freud spawned a host of both loyal and rebellious progeny, whose bitter internecine quarrels over the theory and technique of psychoanalysis are rooted precisely in the question of how to read Freud. Among them we find first of all the fierce defenders of the Freudian legacy, whose most prominent representative was his daughter Anna, a pioneer in the analysis of children. Whilst Anna remained in London after Freud's death, many of his Jewish Viennese disciples took refuge from Nazism in North America, which thereby became associated with the preservation of strict Freudian doctrine, and in particular of his later clinical emphasis on the education and reinforcement of the patient's *ego* (hence the term 'ego-psychology').

Orthodox Freudianism was in some ways entrenched by the emergence of the troublesome 'revisionists', associated above all with Melanie Klein. Klein emigrated in 1926 from Budapest to London, where she effected a profound shift of focus in psychoanalytic inquiry from Freud's Oedipal triangle of mother, father and child, to the pre-Oedipal dyad of mother and baby, between whom she revealed wordless but tempestuous dramas of love and hate. Klein's new emphases gave rise in turn to the British 'object–relations' school represented by the likes of Wilfred Bion and D. W. Winnicott, and so-called because of their conception of selfhood as relational rather than (as it sometimes appears in Freud) enclosed.

Finally, we find the most puzzling (in all senses) of all Freud's descendants: Jacques Lacan, a French analyst who proclaimed a 'return to Freud' against what he saw as the twin distortions of ego-psychological 'orthodoxy' and Kleinian revisionism, and whose clinical innovations (notably the introduction of variable-length psychoanalytic sessions) led to his eventual ejection from the International Psychoanalytic Association. Lacan's tantalizing 'return' was in fact a radical reinterpretation of Freud in the light of structural linguistics, emphasizing the irreducibly duplicitous and destabilizing force of words in generating psychoanalytic 'truth'. Arguably the most widely practiced form of psychoanalysis today, and undoubtedly one of the most influential, Lacan's thought nevertheless continues to occupy an uneasy position at the edge of its institutional boundaries.

This necessarily sketchy account of analysis after Freud (which takes no account of the two major 'secessionists' from the psychoanalytic movement, Alfred Adler and Carl Jung), is intended less as a potted history than as an intimation of the inherent risk one takes in writing a book entitled *How to*

Read Freud. My way of dealing with this risk has been straight-forward: I've simply made no attempt either to elaborate or to adjudicate between the various strains of post-Freudian psychoanalysis, a task well beyond the remit of a short intro-duction to Freud. I have only made reference to other analytic thinkers where they help illuminate a specific point in Freud's work. I've been less sparing, however, in my use of non-analytic sources, from literature and philosophy to advertisement cam-paigns and comic strips – psychoanalysis, after all, is a way of read-ing everything.

My aim in these ten short commentaries has been, above all, to show how rich, complex and curious the inner life becomes under Freud's piercing gaze. Whether addressing neuroses, perversions, slips of the tongue, dreams, jokes, the analytic session, love (of oneself or another), or death, I've tried to show that his exhilarating and infuriating achievement is to deprive all our words and actions, however apparently trivial or straightforward, of their transparency. After Freud, we can no longer simply assume the meaning of anything we say or do: we are forced rather into reading it, and into the risk that our reading may yield nothing like the 'truth'. The reading of Freud's own texts, infinitely elusive in spite of their remarkable clarity, can never be exempt from this rule. One principle to be inferred from my account of how to read Freud is that one should renounce any claim on authority over how to read Freud.

In saying this I don't want to give the impression that there's no such thing as an accurate, or indeed inaccurate, reading of Freud. My point is rather that if a reading is to be accurate, it has to recognise that Freud's thought, in spite of the nineteenth-century register of scientific certainty in which it is couched, begins with the acknowledgement of the *unconscious* – that zone of experience which dissolves all pretensions to stable and certain knowledge.

A Note on Sources

My selection of extracts is taken from James Strachey's famous *Standard Edition of the Complete Psychological Works of Sigmund Freud*, reprinted in paperback by Vintage in 2001. The main and simple reason for this is that it's the only widely available translation of Freud containing all his published (as well as some early unpublished) writings on psychology. I have, however, made a single but decisive change in the translation, in conformity with most post-Strachey translators and commentators: for the German *Trieb* I've consistently substituted 'drive' for Strachey's 'instinct'. I explain this change in more detail in Chapter Seven. For now, suffice it to note that 'instinct' connotes the programmed response of the animal to a given stimulus, 'drive' the always variable and unpredictable response of the human.

References to the *Standard Edition* are denoted throughout this book in parentheses by *SE*, followed by the relevant volume and page numbers. Referencing is omitted where the citation is from the chosen extract.

1

HYSTERICAL BEGINNINGS

Emma is subject at the present time to a compulsion of not being able to go into shops *alone*. As a reason for this [she produced] a memory from the time when she was twelve years old (shortly after puberty). She went into a shop to buy something, saw the two shop-assistants (one of whom she can remember) laughing together, and ran away in some kind of *affect of fright*. In connection with this, she was led to recall that the two of them were laughing at her clothes, and that one of them had pleased her sexually.

The relation of these fragments [to one another] and the effect of the experience are alike unintelligible. If she felt unpleasure at her clothes being laughed at, that must have been corrected long ago, ever since she has been dressing as a [grown-up] lady. Moreover, it makes no difference to her clothes whether she goes into a shop alone or in company. That she is not simply in need of protection is shown by the fact that, as happens with agoraphobia, even the company of a small child is enough to make her feel safe. And there is the quite incongruous fact that one of them pleased her; it would make no difference to this either, if she were accompanied. Thus the memories aroused explain neither the compulsion nor the determination of the symptom.

Further investigation now revealed a second memory, which she denies having had in mind at the moment of Scene I. Nor is there anything to prove this. On two occasions when she was a child of eight she had gone into a small shop to buy some sweets, and the shopkeeper had grabbed at her genitals through her clothes. In spite of the first experience she had gone there a second time; after the second time she stopped away. She now reproached herself for having gone there the second time, as though she had wanted that way to provoke the assault. In fact a state of 'oppressive bad conscience' is to be traced back to this experience.

We now understand Scene I (shop-assistants) if we take Scene II (shopkeeper) along with it. We only need an associative link between the two. She herself pointed out that it was provided by the *laughing*; this laughing of the shop-assistants had reminded her of the grin with which the shopkeeper had accompanied his assault. The course of events can now be reconstructed as follows. In the shop the two assistants were *laughing*; this laughing aroused (unconsciously) the memory of the shopkeeper. Indeed the situation had yet another similarity [to the earlier one]: she was once again in a shop alone. Together with the shopkeeper she remembered his grabbing her through her clothes; but since then she had reached puberty. The memory aroused what it was certainly not able to at the time, a *sexual release*, which was transformed into anxiety. With this anxiety, she was afraid that the shop-assistants might repeat the assault, and she ran away. [. . .] What happened can be represented thus: (see diagram opposite)

Of course, these blacked-in ideas are perceptions which are also remembered. The fact that the sexual release too entered consciousness is proved by the otherwise incomprehensible idea that the laughing shop-assistant had pleased her. The outcome – not to remain in the shop alone on account of the danger of

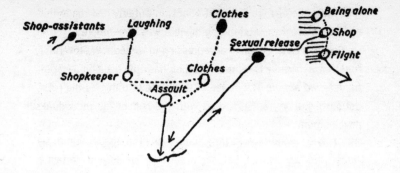

assault – is quite rationally constructed having regard to all the pieces of the associative process. However, nothing of the processes entered consciousness except the element clothes; and the thought operating *consciously* has made two false connections in the material at its disposal (shop-assistants, laughing, clothes, sexual feeling): that she was being laughed at on account of her clothes and that one of the shop-assistants excited sexual pleasure in her. [. . .]

It might be said that it is quite usual, as happens here, for an association to pass through unconscious intermediate links until it comes to a conscious one. In that case, the element which enters consciousness is probably the one that arouses special interest. In our example, however, it is noticeable precisely that the element which enters consciousness is not the one that arouses interest (assault) but another one, as a symbol (clothes). If we ask ourselves what may be the cause of the interpolated pathological process, only one presents itself – the *sexual release*, of which there is also evidence in consciousness. This is linked to the memory of the assault; but it is highly noteworthy that it [the sexual release] was not linked to the assault when this was experienced. Here we have the case of a memory arousing an affect which it did not arouse as an experience, because in the

meantime the change [brought about] in puberty had made possible a different understanding of what was remembered.

   Now this case is typical of repression in hysteria. We invariably
find that a memory is repressed which has only become a trauma
by *deferred action*. The cause of this state of things is the retar-
dation of puberty as compared with the rest of the individual's
development.

Extract from 'Project for a Scientific Psychology', SE 1, pp.
353–6

A mysterious compulsion; memories of a humiliation that
aroused desire and of abuse that induced shame: Freud is led
by Emma's tantalizing trail of neurotic symptoms and traumatic memories into the deepest enigmas of mental life.

   At first glance there's something almost comically excessive
about Emma's phobic reaction to shops, more accentuated
than diminished by the memory she calls up in association
with it, of being simultaneously laughed at and sexually
pleased. With a leap of sympathetic imagination, the fright
induced at the time by the shop assistants' laughter is just
about intelligible; but that this fright should have persisted
into adult life, extending itself in the process to all shops,
seems to affront our sense of emotional proportion.

   There is something of a tacit bad faith amongst us enlight-
ened moderns that the Newtonian logic of equal and opposite
reactions should extend from the physical to the emotional.
Isn't this what we try to instil in our children – that screams
and tears aren't warranted by the refusal of a lollipop? This is
the first and fundamental law of mental life that Freud elaborates in the 'Project': the function of the mind, or rather, 'the
nervous system' (the 'Project' is couched in neurological
rather than psychological terms) is 'to avoid being burdened

by Qη [that is, the quantity of internal stimulus] or to keep the burden as small as possible' (*SE* 1, p. 301). It's this function we seek to cultivate in children: 'Don't over-excite yourself!' and 'It'll end in tears!' translate into the child's idiom, 'Keep your burden of Qη as small as possible!'

Indeed, as if to underline its primacy, Freud models this function on the hungry baby. Faced with a side view of its mother's breast which obscures the desired nipple, the baby recalls that turning its head recovers the frontal view which enables it to feed. Such primitive training by memory is Freud's evidence of the fundamentally 'economic' nature of the mind. The elaborate wiring of our nervous system is designed to uphold this economy of stimulus by keeping its flow as low and even as possible. It's hard to overstate the centrality of this principle to his thought. From these early formulations in the 'Project' to the speculations on the 'death-drive' some twenty-five years later, the principle of economy structures Freud's picture of the mind.

It is this principle that Emma's phobia seems to offend. Why does she expend such a disproportionate quantity of energy? If she had a bad experience in one shop, why not avoid that shop rather than shops in general? If she experienced the fright at puberty, why does it still possess her as an adult? And why, as Freud himself asks, do the details of her clothing and her need for company in shops take on such significance? The suggestion implicit in these usefully naïve questions is that Emma is making life unnecessarily unpleasant for herself. And the suggestion is instructive when we consider the name Freud would give to the principle of mental economy: the *pleasure principle*. The mind's first and last imperative is to avoid 'unpleasure' (*Unlust* – Freud's coinages often sound alien in the English language); it does so by discharging unwanted excess of stimulus – as hunger is discharged by eating, fatigue by sleep and sexual desire by orgasm. The avoidance of a place, person or even an idea that have painful associations for us conforms to the same principle. Hence our ability to understand Emma's avoidance of entering the offending shop alone, but our bewilderment before her compulsion to spread her fear so far into space and time: avoidance of the one shop for some time would show obedience to the pleasure principle, yet avoiding every shop for all time suggests a self-defeating indifference to it.

A clarification and development of the pleasure principle may be in order at this point. First, the clarification: obedience to the pleasure principle is tied intimately to the imperative of discharge. What this means in practice is that Freud defines pleasure in terms of its ends rather than its means. Pleasure is experienced in the relief of being satiated rather than in the act of eating or sex. Indeed for Freud, undue fixation on the means at the expense of the ends of sexual behaviour is the core of perversion. We shall have occasion later to question this rather mechanistic distinction between the means and ends of pleasure.

Second, the development should be explained. Freud would come to identify a second principle – the *reality principle* – which modifies and subdues the first. From birth, the child is in thrall to pleasure, to the libidinal *drives* (*Triebe*) that scream from within for satisfaction. Experience, however, and the discipline of his elders, teaches him that these untamed libidinal demands are self-defeating and potentially self-destructive. From the relatively trivial discovery that if he tries to eat too many sweets he'll be made sick, to the more fundamental and traumatizing one that if he tries to possess his beloved mother, his father will frustrate (or even – but this is for later – castrate) him, he discovers that life places unending obstacles in between the desire for and the fulfilment of pleasure. This process is essentially a slow and reluctant shift of allegiance from the pleasure to the reality principle.

This shift shouldn't be seen as simple renunciation; on the contrary, says Freud, in his 1911 essay, 'The Two Principles of Mental Functioning', 'the substitution of the reality principle for the pleasure principle implies no deposing of the pleasure principle, but only a safeguarding of it' (*SE* 12, p. 223). The precarious rush of instant gratification gives way to the more secure and measured satisfactions of postponement.

As hinted, a key moment of this shift occurs with the child's acceptance of the impossibility of his sexual desire, for which he is neither biologically prepared nor socially licensed. This acceptance gives rise to the onset around the child's fifth year of what Freud calls the *latency* period, whereby his libidinal drives are *repressed* until – around puberty – they allow of the possibility of satisfaction. This two-stage model of sexual development, unique to the human animal, should shed some light on the enigmas of Emma's hysteria.

The failure of Emma's first memory adequately to account for the force of her compulsion leads her to a second memory from her ninth year, in which she went into a sweet shop where the shopkeeper grabbed her genitals through her clothes. She retraces her 'oppressive bad conscience' to her willingness to return to the shop a second time, 'as if she had wanted that way to provoke the assault'.

Freud's subsequent unravelling of the threads that weave the first scene intricately into the second recalls his chapter in the *Studies on Hysteria* on 'The Psychotherapy of Hysteria', in which he traced hysterical symptoms to pathogenic or psychically toxic ideas 'of a kind that one would prefer not to have experienced, that one would rather forget' (*SE* 2, p. 269). So intolerable are these ideas that a portion of the mind feels compelled to mount a defence against their direct expression. No defence, however, can make the idea disappear; what it can do is to divert and displace the thought, or as Freud puts it in the 'Project', 'direct the cathexis [*Besetzung*, literally charge or investment] of attention *elsewhere*' (*SE* 1, p. 382).

The apparent anomalies of both 'scenes' should by now be less glaring. First of all why, to address a topical question, did the eight-year-old Emma return to the shop? The two-stage theory of sexuality should provide a clue here. In the words of the 'Project', 'no sexual experiences produce any effect so long as the subject is ignorant of all sexual feeling – in general, that is, till the beginning of puberty' (*SE* 1, p. 333). Emma is in the midst of latency – her infantile libido has been driven underground, and she is some years off its adolescent revival.[3] In this phase of what we might call unconsciously willed ignorance, the child experiences the sexual approach as unintelligible – an alien force invading a body incapable of making sense of it. When Freud claims that 'no sexual experiences produce any effect' in those ignorant of sexual feeling, he is far from suggesting that the sexual abuse of children in latency is harmless. Rather, he is pointing to the radical inability of the child to register such feeling other than as a frighteningly opaque enigma. If Emma returns to the scene of her abuse, it is perhaps in the hope of rendering it more intelligible, and so less threatening; the return, therefore, is a necessarily confused mode of defence. And an inevitably failed defence: instead of resolving the frightful strangeness of the assault, her return reinforces it, inducing the insistent shame or 'oppressive bad conscience' that has never gone away.

Freud's diagram of the relationship between the two scenes

enables us to see the excessive nature of Emma's reaction to the second scene as a distorted mirror image of the insufficiency of her reaction to the first scene. In terms of the principle of psychic economy, this mirroring is very significant – placed in relation to the earlier scene, Emma's phobia loses its excessive appearance and becomes instead an attempt to restore the economy so violently disturbed by the shopkeeper's assault. The phobia, that is, becomes a means of containing and redistributing the overload of stimulus he introduced into her nervous system.

In this respect, the mechanism of displacement, about which we'll hear a lot more in the next chapter, is an indispensable agent for maintaining psychical economy. Here is the 'Project's description of this mechanism:

> There has been an occurrence which consisted of B+A. A was an incidental circumstance; B was appropriate for producing the lasting effect. The reproduction of this event in memory has now taken a form of such a kind that it is as though A had stepped into B's place. Hence the incongruity: A is accompanied by consequences which it does not seem worthy of, which do not fit in with it. (SE 1, p. 349)

The overriding effect of displacement is *incongruity*. Displacement transfers the charge from an intolerable to an indifferent or 'incidental' memory, investing the latter with an *Unlust* that it doesn't seem to warrant. Thus, the relatively trivial laughter of the shop assistants in the later scene becomes an insidious disguise for the first shopkeeper's grin. As such, it triggers the fright that couldn't find expression in the earlier scene. Similarly, the recurring motif of clothing magnetizes the traumatic effect of the earlier assault to the mild humiliation of the later scene. In hysteria, as in the other neuroses, and indeed all of the psychological phenomena which psychoanalysis would come to explore, the (intolerable) truth typically appears in the guise of the (tolerably) trivial.

But the key element enabling the transformation of the later into a distorted version of the earlier scene is Emma's sexual pleasure at the sight of the assistant. The now pubescent Emma is able to register the sexual desire inaccessible to her in latency. Filtered through the common motifs of shops, clothing and laughter, the sexual pleasure of Scene I repeats in distorted form the sexual violation of Scene II. Emma's fright at her own desire is, to use Freud's term from the end of this passage, *nachträglich* – an 'after-blow', a deferred response to what had allowed of no response in its original, traumatic occurrence.

The significance of this after-blow can be gleaned from an apparently trivial detail of Freud's presentation – the labelling of the *earlier* event as Scene II. This is partly explained by his clinical observation in the *Studies* that the memories precipitating a hysteria are typically recalled in reverse chronological order. But this fails to account for why Freud declines to restore the 'correct' order in his reconstruction. The answer might be that in a very important sense this *is* the correct order. As long as the later scene hasn't occurred, the earlier scene has no psychological reality for Emma – from the perspective of the inner life, rather than external reality, the later memory gives birth to the earlier one. Time in the mind is truly out of joint.

2

THE UN*CON*SCIOUS

THE SPECIAL CHARACTERISTICS OF THE SYSTEM *UCS*

The distinction we have made between the two psychical systems
receives fresh significance when we observe that processes in the
one system, the *Ucs.*[4], show characteristics which are not met
with again in the system immediately above it.

The nucleus of the *Ucs.* consists of drive-representatives
which seek to discharge their cathexes; that is to say, it consists
of wishful impulses. These drive-impulses are co-ordinate with
one another, exist side by side without being influenced by one
another, and are exempt from mutual contradiction. When two
wishful impulses whose aims must appear to us incompatible
become simultaneously active, the two impulses do not diminish
each other or cancel each other out, but combine to form an
intermediate aim, a compromise.

There are in this system no negation, no doubt, no degrees of
certainty: all this is only introduced by the work of the censorship
between the *Ucs.* and the *Pcs.* Negation is a substitute, at a
higher level, for repression. In the *Ucs.*, there are only contents,
cathected with greater or lesser strength.

The cathected intensities [in the *Ucs.*] are much more mobile. By the process of *displacement* one idea may surrender to another its whole quota of cathexis; by the process of *condensation* it may appropriate the whole cathexis of several other ideas. I have proposed to regard these two processes as distinguishing marks of the so-called *primary psychical process.* In the system *Pcs.* the *secondary process* is dominant. When a primary process is allowed to take its course in connection with elements belonging to the system *Pcs.*, it appears 'comic' and excites laughter.

The processes of the system *Ucs.* are *timeless,* i.e. they are not ordered temporally, are not altered by the passage of time; they have no reference to time at all. Reference to time is bound up, once again, with the work of the system *Cs.*

The *Ucs.* processes pay just as little regard to *reality.* They are subject to the pleasure principle; their fate depends only on how strong they are and on whether they fulfil the demands of the pleasure-unpleasure regulation.

To sum up: *exemption from mutual contradiction, primary process* (mobility of cathexes), *timelessness,* and *replacement of external by psychical reality* – these are the characteristics which we may expect to find in the processes belonging to the system *Ucs.*

Extract from 'The Unconscious', *SE* 14, pp. 186–7

With this passage from 'The Unconscious', the longest and most demanding of Freud's five 1915 'Papers on Metapsychology', we take a twenty year leap forward. But this historical distance from the 'Project' is matched by some striking theoretical continuities.

One example of such continuity can be found in the lone bracket at the base of the earlier passage's diagram illustrating the relation between the two 'scenes'. Look at the diagram, and note that this bracket represents the source from which all Emma's symptoms (the phobia, the mysterious sexual release) arise, and into which the associated memories run back. And yet, alone of all the graphic markers in the diagram, the bracket has no verbal tag, as if there's no word to designate what it represents. It seems that whilst the disparate symptoms, affects and memories through which Emma's neurosis manifests itself can be observed and classified, their enigmatic source cannot.

This apparently marginal observation about the earlier diagram might help make sense of the later passage. What we find in the diagram is an anticipation in visual form of Freud's distinction between the 'two psychical systems' at the outset of the later passage. Even the spatial terms of the diagram are transposed to the later text: just as in the former the manifestations of the neurosis are placed above their source, so in the latter the 'preconscious' system is placed above the 'unconscious'. Much more than a figure of speech, this conception of the mind as a dynamic of manifest phenomena 'above' and latent contents 'below' defined Freud's first model or topography of the mind.

The extract offers a formidably compressed description of the lower level of this topography – better known of course as the unconscious (*das Unbewusste*) or in Freud's technical abbreviation, *Ucs.* (*Ubw*). Indeed, first impressions would suggest that the earlier text's reticence about naming and describing this lower stratum of the mind has been overcome. In place of the diagram's mute graphic symbol is a comprehensive and technically precise elucidation of 'the special characteristics of the system *Ucs*'. Yet for all its specialized vocabulary, can we say that the passage succeeds in pinning down its object scientifically? Isn't there a striking mismatch between the precision of the vocabulary and the obscurity of the entity it describes?

The processes that characterize the unconscious, he tells us, aren't met with in the system above it: the *preconscious (das Vorbewusste)*, or *Pcs.* (*Vbw.*). The preconscious is the stream of memories and perceptions to which the *conscious (das Bewusste)*, or *Cs.* (*Bw.*) has ready access. For example, when I alight upon a single face in the midst of a rapidly streaming crowd, I pass from preconscious to conscious perception. The preconscious designates what is potentially available, the conscious what is actually present, to the mind. Together they constitute the secondary process of mental life.

In contrast, the unconscious, as the name suggests, is precisely that region of mental life to which consciousness has no ready access. As such, it is inaccessible to positive description. Freud's statement that its processes 'show characteristics which are not met with again in the system immediately above it' might be restated thus: *unconscious processes cannot be captured in the language of conscious ones*. The consequences of this predicament are made very apparent in the extract.

Take the first 'special characteristic' of the unconscious Freud identifies: 'it consists of drive-representatives [*Triebrepräsentanzen*] which seek to discharge their cathexes; that is to say, it consists of wishful impulses'. In less technical terms: the unconscious is the domain of the unrestricted pleasure principle, an underground cavern of drives demanding perpetual satisfaction, drives so imperious they are oblivious to one another's presence: 'Drive impulses . . . exist side by side without being influenced by one another, and are exempt from mutual contradiction'. The dry, quasi-scientific vocabulary can't conceal – indeed only accentuates – the disturbing indeterminacy of the object it describes. Freud

employs the authoritative tone of the man of science to delin-
eate an entity beyond the reach of direct classification and
observation.

How, then, are we to understand a force that violates
(common) sense? A proverbial illustration may be helpful: I
can of course desire both to have my cake and to eat it. But to
be conscious is to know that discharging one of these desires
cancels out the other. The unconscious does not know this: its
desires both to possess and to consume the cake can exist side
by side, blissfully impervious to their basic incompatibility. In
the unconscious, I eat my cake and continue to demand I
have it – not however, *another* cake, but precisely *that* cake, the
one I've eaten.

The key to this stubborn irrationality is given in the two
penultimate paragraphs in the passage: the unconscious, we
are told, knows neither time nor reality. Only the experience
of time's duration enables us to connect eating the cake to the
impossibility of having it: what I have eaten belongs to the
past; it is no longer mine to have. Only the ability to accom-
modate reality – the most basic discipline, we recall from the
last chapter, that a child undergoes – teaches me that what is
destroyed cannot continue to exist. As Freud himself noted
more than once, experience is governed by what Kant called,
'the necessary forms of thought' (*SE* 18, p. 28): the laws of
space and time. Freud's corrective to Kant, however, is to
confine the rule of these laws to *conscious* experience, and to
posit a formless region of mental life where these laws don't
hold sway, where 'there are only contents'.

Is it, then, the case that these contents without form can
break into our conscious language only as literal non-sense (as
in, 'give me the cake I have just eaten')? Not quite, the passage
tells us. There are two processes in the unconscious which

bring these contents to conscious expression, the first of which, displacement, we have already come across, and the second is *condensation*. Rather than enter into the detail of how these processes work, I want to begin from a more elementary observation: displacement and condensation are disguises, ways of expressing indirectly what cannot be expressed directly. If we return for the last time to the 'Emma' diagram, we can see how it gives visual expression to this logic of disguise: the nameless bracket is nothing more than a repository of amorphous contents. This inarticulate chaos of the inner life can't be expressed as it is; it can find expression only in displacements and condensations. Thus, the unconscious fears and desires associated with the enigma of sexuality are displaced, or 'surrendered to', the conscious image of 'clothes'. Meanwhile the dual appearance of 'clothes' and 'laughter' in each scene enables the process of condensation, whereby one idea in the unconscious 'may appropriate the cathexis of several other ideas'. Thus for Emma, the affects of fright, shame and sexual pleasure are condensed in the single motif of clothing. Shops, shop assistants, clothes, laughter: whatever that bracket contains can be accessed only through these disguises.

We never know the unconscious other than through its disguises. Aware that such a formulation, notwithstanding the illustrative support from Emma, may seem forbiddingly abstract, I want to enlist the help of a novel. The intention in so doing isn't to subject it or its author, Herman Melville, to a 'Freudian' reading; on the contrary, the question is more what Freud and his unconscious look like in Melville's bewitching light.

Published in 1857, *The Confidence Man*[5], Melville's ninth novel in eleven years, threw his already ailing reputation into freefall. Reading it today, it's not difficult to guess at what alienated its contemporaries: for all its airy comedy and playfulness, there's a void at its heart which even after a 150-year interval of modernist experiment remains profoundly disconcerting: the void of the titular protagonist himself.

The novel is set on April Fool's Day aboard a Mississippi steamer with the wittily allegorical name of *Fidèle*, and begins with the boarding at St Louis of a deaf-mute in a cream-coloured suit: 'in the extremest sense of the word, a stranger'. The stranger proceeds to a placard 'offering a reward for the capture of a mysterious impostor', and brandishes beside it a slate on which he has written 'Charity thinketh no evil'. His subsequent passive refusal to stand aside and clear a passage renders the crowd increasingly hostile, until he is forced to escape to the upper deck, where he retires to sleep – disappearing from the novel in the process.

In the following chapter, a black cripple, Guinea, provokes a furious argument between members of the crowd as to whether he is as he appears, or, as one man claims, really a white conman milking the crowd's credulousness. By the chapter's end, Guinea has weathered the quarrelsome storm around him and shamed a guilty white merchant into a half-dollar donation.

Sequences of chapters follow, in each of which a new character is introduced who induces in a new interlocutor a similar shift from mistrust to self-reproach, from scepticism to credulousness. And the culmination of each sequence is reassuringly repetitious: money is handed over nervously, enthusiastically or piously by the one to the other. What we are witnessing, we gradually realise, is a series of con-tricks perpetrated by the same individual in different and impenetrable disguises.

So far we seem to have the makings of a eccentric

entertainment, anticipating Twain or O. Henry rather more than Freud. But Melville's novel leapfrogs these later writers and into the heart of modernism by way of a narrative twist at once bizarre and startlingly simple. Told by a less perverse (and less brilliant) writer, the story would pivot on the revelation of the conman's real identity – perhaps on his failed or successful attempts to evade capture, or on his base or noble motives for mass deception. We wait in vain for any such moment in *The Confidence Man*. Some way into the novel the penny drops: there is to be no unmasking of the 'real' conman, only the potentially infinite proliferation of his masks. The confidence man never appears other than in and as (this is the novel's subtitle) 'His Masquerade'. Indeed, beyond his disguises, the confidence man does not exist.

I am of course evoking my formulation above: we never know the unconscious other than through its disguises. The unconscious is a confidence man in this sense above all: we have no access to its unadorned reality, but only to its masks, its displacements and condensations, 'distinguishing marks of the so-called *primary psychical process*'. Try to pull away the masks, and, like the confidence man, it will simply evaporate.

'Everything profound loves a mask', wrote Nietzsche in 1886, as Freud was turning his interests to psychotherapy. Freud would later confess to his avoidance of reading Nietzsche, 'whose guesses and intuitions often agree in the most astonishing way with the laborious findings of psychoanalysis' (*SE* 20, p. 60), for fear of compromising the originality of his own thought. The contrasting terms of the sentence reveal the paradox of his affinity with Nietzsche (among many others): Freud follows the 'laborious' paths of exact science and yet in so doing confirms the most audacious radical 'guesses and intuitions' of the philosophers and poets.

It's a commonplace notion that Freud conferred the dignity of scientific legitimacy on the poet's intuitions; more expectedly, but just as strikingly, psychoanalysis coaxes science into affirming the dense ambiguities of art. If writing about Freud evokes irresistibly the spirits of Melville, Nietzsche and so many others, it's because his thought, for all its rigour and precision, turns on an enigma it cannot pin down. The quest for the truth of mental life culminates in the same paradox as the quest for the confidence man's true identity: 'everything profound loves a mask'. The truth of human beings is found *in* their masks, not behind them.

Of course, the unconscious is a confidence man in a stricter sense too. Its relations with the two systems above it are not unlike those of the conman to his fellow passengers. If the conman revealed his deepest impulses to his victims, he wouldn't be a conman; expressed directly, his wishes to attain power over and extract money from them would be entirely self-defeating. To be effective, he must disguise those wishes as abject supplication, pious altruism, canny commercialism – anything other than, 'I want your money'. The conman works by enlisting his victims as unwitting co-conspirators in their own deception.

Recall that in his first appearance, the conman is, 'in the extremest sense of the word a stranger': a deaf-mute bearing a slate enjoining the crowd to 'charity'. It is the only guise in which he doesn't attempt to extract money from others. On the contrary, he is hounded off the deck, retreating into sleep and 'disappearing' undetected. Extreme strangeness provokes intense suspicion, especially, Freud would observe in a later work, in groups. In order to insinuate himself into the body of passengers, the conman has to conjure away this strangeness, to make it disappear. Indeed, one of his first cons involves convincing his puzzled and embarrassed victim that they're old acquaintances. In a successful con, the stranger breaks down the suspicion he provokes by assuming the guise of the familiar.

The unconscious has to perform similar ruses in order to gain entry into the conscious. When an unconscious idea makes itself known, its strangeness may provoke its conscious counterpart, like the angry passengers, to beat it back into oblivion. Freud's own analogy in his *Five Lectures on Psychoanalysis* of 1911 is very instructive here: imagine, he told his audience, that among you is, 'someone who is caus- ing a disturbance' with his 'ill-mannered laughter, chattering and shuffling with his feet' (*SE* 11, p. 25). The 'interrupter' is ejected, and chairs are jammed against the door to block his re-entry. Freud was using the metaphor to explain the process of repression – an intolerable idea is banished by the conscious mind, and a resistance set up against its return.

But of course, removing a person from a room doesn't do away with him: the unconscious idea continues to exist after its repression. Banned from the main entrance, the interrupter must find some other way to maintain his presence. One way, as Freud noted, is to shout and bang on the door with his fists. It is the way of the neurotic, whose symptoms – hysteria, obsessive compulsions, melancholia – behave like the banging fists of an idea that the conscious 'audience' has refused or been unable to hear directly.

But this isn't the way of the confidence man. He deals with being ejected by slipping back in as someone else, some- one less suspiciously strange. Rather than set himself outside of the company, he will make an exaggerated claim to be one of them, and so enlist them surreptitiously to his own devious ends. This, in fact, is how the unconscious insinuates itself into the everyday mental life of us all, in the form of *dreams* (the focus of our next chapter) and *parapraxes*. These latter – 'forgetting, slips of the tongue, bungled actions, superstitions and errors' – provide eloquent testimony to the concealed presence of the unconscious in daily life. Freud's *The Psychopathology of Everyday Life*, one of the most popular books in his corpus, is a compendium (in truth a rather tedious one), built up over countless editions, of material of this kind. To select one nicely compact example from the hundreds available: a gentleman tells a lady at an evening party about the beautiful display of flowers in Wertheim's department store: 'The place is completely *decollated*' (*SE* 6, p. 70).

The etiquette of cocktail party mingling doesn't generally allow for expressions of predatory admiration for a woman's *décolletage*, which may have earned their speaker anything from a rebuke to ejection from the party. Aware that its lustful impulse can't attain direct entry into the conversation, the unconscious 'slips' it in under the cover of an innocuous sound-alike. In this way, the very polite interaction which was intended to guard social norms is enlisted by the unconscious in the service of its transgression. An admirable con: the unconscious makes a friend of the unsuspecting word 'decorated' and thereby gets the conscious to do its own nefarious work. An instance of the process described by Freud in the passage discussed in this chapter, whereby two contradictory wishes 'do not diminish each other or cancel each other out, but combine to form an intermediate aim, a compromise'. Giving expression to the strange primary under cover of the familiar secondary process, these slips are the very spirit of compromise.

It is worth noting one final feature as a prelude to the consideration of dreams, the most elaborate of compromises.

Slips tend to be funny, in accordance with the rule that, 'When a primary process is allowed to take its course in connection with elements belonging to the system *Pcs.*, it appears "comic" and excites laughter'. What is it about the elaborate ruses of the unconscious, about the tortuous means by which it wends its way into conscious life, that makes us laugh?

3

UNCONSCIOUS WIT – DREAMS

A young man, whose door-bell had been rung late one night by an acquaintance who wanted to leave a visiting-card on him, had a dream that night: *A man had been working till late in the evening to put his house-telephone in order. After he had gone, it kept on ringing – not continuously, but with detached rings. His servant fetched the man back, and the latter remarked: 'It's a funny thing that even people who are "tutelrein" as a rule are quite unable to deal with a thing like this.'*

It will be seen that the indifferent exciting cause of the dream only covers one element of it. The episode only obtained any importance from the fact that the dreamer put it in the same series as an earlier experience which, though equally indifferent in itself, was given a substitutive meaning by his imagination. When he was a boy, living with his father, he had upset a glass of water over the floor while he was half-asleep. The flex of the house-telephone had been soaked through and its *continuous ringing* had disturbed his father's sleep. Since the continuous ringing corresponded to getting wet, the *'detached rings'* were used to represent drops falling. The word *'tutelrein'* could be analysed in three directions, and led in that way to three of the subjects represented in the dream-thoughts. *'Tutel'* is a legal term for 'guardianship' ['tutelage']. *'Tutel'* (or possibly *'Tuttel'*) is also a vulgar term for a woman's breast. The remaining portion of the word, *'rein'* ['clean'], combined with the first part of *'Zimmertelegraph'* ['house-telephone'], forms *'zimmerrein'* ['house-trained'] – which is closely connected with making the floor wet, and, in addition, sounded very much like the name of a member of the dreamer's family.

In waking life this same kind of analysis and synthesis of syllables – a syllabic chemistry, in fact – plays a part in a great number of jokes [. . .] The first reader and critic of this book – and his successors are likely to follow his example – protested that 'the dreamer seems to be too ingenious and amusing'. This is quite true so long as it refers only to the dreamer; it would only be an objection if it were to be extended to the dream-interpreter. In waking reality I have little claim to be regarded as a wit. If my dreams seem amusing, that is not on my account, but on account of the peculiar psychological conditions under which dreams are constructed; and the fact is intimately connected with the theory of jokes and the comic. Dreams become ingenious and amusing because the direct and easiest pathway to the expression of their thoughts is barred: they are forced into being so. The reader can convince himself that my patients' dreams seem at least as full of jokes and puns as my own, or even fuller.

Extract from *The Interpretation of Dreams*, SE 4, pp. 297–8

Why, to recall the puzzle that emerged at the end of the previous chapter, are we provoked to laughter by the bubbling of unconscious processes to the surface of the mind? Central to Freud's inquiries from the outset, this question was instrumental in shaping and directing the psychoanalytic enterprise. Should this claim sound far-fetched, consider each of the phenomena anatomized in the triad of books through which he disseminated his new science – dreams (*The Interpretation of Dreams*, 1900); errors (*The Psychopathology of Everyday Life*, 1901); and jokes (*Jokes and Their Relation to the Unconscious*, 1905). They reveal the intrusions of the unconscious as a common source of everyday laughter. If, as discussed in the last chapter, repression drives the primary processes of the unconscious into hiding, then dreams, errors and jokes are their comical means of breaking cover. They are ruses of the unconscious, elaborate escape routes ingeniously burrowed out of the dungeon of repression.

So after the forward leap into 'The Unconscious', let us take a backward one into *The Interpretation of Dreams* (*Die Traumdeutung*), the founding and in many ways unsurpassed text of psychoanalytic theory. Our fragment of dream analysis and its accompanying footnote reveal the mysterious 'syllabic chemistry' by which unconscious impulses precipitate laughter. If the unconscious is waging a perpetual clandestine war against the sovereignty of the conscious, laughter is its most potent chemical weapon.

Organised around the famous premise that, 'The interpretation of dreams is the royal road to a knowledge of the unconscious activities of the mind' (*SE* 5, p. 608), Freud's book identified the elaborately nonsensical 'work' of the sleeping mind, hitherto marginalized and trivialized by science, as the key to the function and structure of all mental life. How is it that dreams promise so much to the seeker of psychological truth?

In the last chapter we discovered how unconscious impulses, barred by repression from direct entry into the auditorium of consciousness, can slip in under verbal cover. Thus, the young man's sensitive admiration for the display of flowers ('decorated') provided the unconscious with an ideal vehicle for expressing his admiration for a rather different display ('decollated'). Slips are, well, slippery: they sneak into the auditorium undetected, merging seamlessly with the line of legitimate ticket-holders as a well-spoken and smartly dressed friend distracts the usher. But for this same reason, they're essentially harmless. A single rogue spectator, surrounded on all sides by attentive ones, doesn't have much room for manoeuvre. If he makes his presence felt too palpably, he will be summarily banished. He can escape this fate only by reducing himself to near imperceptibility: it's possible the young woman at the party will have heard the intended 'decorated', or simply missed the innuendo effected by the switch of consonants. The triumph of the slip ultimately confirms more than denies the rule of the conscious.

The usher of the waking mind performs his duties zealously, aware of his grave responsibility to ensure that the performance in the auditorium remains undisturbed. If too many inadmissible thoughts sneak past him or, if repression fails, neurotic illness will break out. His night-time substitute, on the other hand, is rather more slack. As anyone who's had a dream knows, it doesn't take much for a thought to get into one. A thought, remember, is directly admitted to the waking mind only when it can demonstrate its obedience to the laws of time and reality. The sleeping mind, it seems, isn't nearly so fastidious. The continuity of time and the solidity of reality, iron laws of the day, are happily dispensable at night. In waking life, our sense of reality is sustained by the capacity to distinguish one thing from another, precisely the capacity lacking in the unconscious, which enjoys the privilege of 'exemption from mutual contradiction'. In dreams, we may well find, we can have the cake we just ate.

Yet we should be wary of designating dreams as the exclusive domain of the unconscious. After all, as well as violating the laws of conscious life, dreams can display a surprising conformity to them. It is tempting but wrong to understand sleep as being under the direct and unchallenged rule of the unconscious. We introduced the conman precisely to point up the impossibility of unconscious processes becoming, in Freud's phase 'conscious as such' (*SE* 5, p. 612). Neither the conman nor the unconscious ever appears 'as such' but only in their multiform disguises. But what the *Traumdeutung* reveals is that dreams provide the unconscious with the richest and most plastic resources for disguising its impulses. No other form of mental activity offers it so much space to explore freely, to give voice, albeit distorted, to those ideas silenced by the conscious.

Nevertheless this freedom is far from absolute. The usher on the night shift may have a more relaxed door policy towards the thoughts seeking entry, but he doesn't abandon rules of admission altogether. Clothing need not be formal, as in the waking mind, where thoughts must conform to a strictly enforced syntactical and logical dress code. But neither can an unconscious impulse turn up naked and expect to be let in. For this usher has a grave responsibility too: he is to ensure that dreams serve their proper function as '*the GUARDIANS of sleep and not its disturbers*' (*SE* 4, p. 233). Dreams are not only outlets for discharging the excess mental stimulus accumulated in the unconscious in the course of the day, they are equally mechanisms for ensuring, in accordance with the pleasure principle, that this discharge is sufficiently low and even to prevent disturbances of sleep.

Dreams are, in other words, responsible for mastering any excitations emanating from the unconscious. The unconscious is opportunistic: it knows that it can get away with a great deal more by night than by day. But it also knows it won't benefit from recklessness. Once the level of mental excitation, painful or pleasurable, is raised past a certain threshold, sleep becomes impossible to preserve. Inasmuch as this results in the restoration of the far more repressive regime of the waking mind, it amounts to a defeat for the unconscious. In dreams, the unconscious is thus impelled by the dual imperative to give expression to its prohibited contents without raising the alarm of the conscious. For if those contents exhibit themselves too obviously, the unconscious will lose the relative freedom bestowed by sleep. Like a good burglar, it's in its interests to avoid waking the owners of the house.

To invoke Freud's earlier metaphor once again, the usher on the day shift is incorruptible. Unconscious impulses won't get past him if he has anything to do with it. His counterpart at night is more flexible – he cuts a deal, or, in Freud's own terminology, he makes a *compromise* with the troublesome unconscious visitors: 'You can come in if you don't make too much noise – that way, I keep my job, and you don't get kicked out.' His attitude is less cynical than realistic. He knows that delinquents need to be indulged a little if they're not to become completely unmanageable. The performers and spectators occupying the auditorium during the day have gone home to rest, leaving the space available for devotees of the edgier, sexually and violently tinged underground art scene. If by morning the space is in more or less the condition they found it, even the daytime usher will turn a blind eye – he too understands the value of the compromise, and indeed that he's one of its beneficiaries. If those unconscious impulses are kept occupied at night, they're less likely to cause him bother during the day.

But we've yet to explain how dreams keep the unconscious from causing too great a disturbance. In attempting to do so, it's helpful to make use of yet another metaphor, this time from *The Interpretation of Dreams* itself. The metaphor is instructive because it points to the affinity of dreams to written language. Dreams, said Freud, like the press under an autocratic regime, are the outcome of a compromise between the reporters of the unconscious and the censor, who monitors and edits the material submitted. But as writers in such regimes have discovered, there are ways of getting around censorship: 'for instance, he may describe a dispute between two Mandarins in the Middle Kingdom, when the people he has in mind are officials in his own country' (*SE* 4, p. 142). Like censored writers, dreams labour under the double imperative to reveal and to conceal their own meanings. They are not intrinsically 'witty and ingenious', as the footnote to our present passage states, but rather 'forced into becoming so' by the fact that, 'the direct and easiest pathway to the expression of their thoughts is barred'. Freud's coinage for this forced wit and ingenuity – the 'dream-work' (*Traumarbeit*) – is very precise: in the absence of a direct and easy pathway to satisfaction, dreams are forced to work, to weave painstaking disguises and make labyrinthine detours. They displace and condense meanings, forge a system of oblique verbal and visual representation to substitute for the more exact vocabulary and syntax of our waking language. Freud noted, for example, that dreams possess no means of representing 'either/or' (in this regard they of course bear the mark of their unconscious sources) other than as vagueness (auditory or visual). That which the waking mind represents as similar, the dreaming mind represents as unified, whilst what we consciously perceive as a logical relation between two entities is figured by the dream by means of simultaneity in time. Painful affects or emotions whose direct expression meet with the censor's marker pen are reversed, as in the dream Freud records in which an elderly gentleman registers his morbid sadness at his impending death, as 'unrestrained laughter' (*SE* 5, p. 473).

But above all, dreams are wily and assiduous exploiters of the intrinsic ambiguity of words. To see them at work, we need only return to the dream of the house-telephone. The dream neatly illustrates Freud's claim that dreams have two sources: 'residues' left in the mind during the preceding day (here the late-night ringing of the doorbell by the dreamer's acquaintance) which shape the dream's manifest content; and unconscious memories and phantasies which the dreamer brings into association with the manifest content during the analytic session. These associations (here the dreamer's boyhood memories) form a path to the dream's latent content, or unconscious meanings.

The first association brought by the dreamer is 'an earlier experience', which he places in series with the 'indifferent exciting cause' of the previous evening's ringing doorbell: as a boy, he had soaked the flex of the house-telephone, causing it to ring continuously and disturb his father's sleep. Insignificant in isolation, the preceding evening's incident is impregnated with meaning by this earlier one. Still, does this mirroring of the later in the earlier incident help resolve the enigma of the dream's meaning? Hardly – on the contrary, the earlier incident is the beginning rather than the end of the chain of association. Just as the dream alludes to the preceding evening's event, which in turn disguises the boyhood experience, so the boyhood incident conceals deeper and more obscure memories and phantasies.

We might say that every displacement only displaces another displacement. That is, interpretation doesn't burrow down to an ultimate kernel of unconscious material which reveals the full and incontestable meaning of the dream. On the contrary, Freud wrote:

> There is often a passage in even the most thoroughly interpreted dream which has to be left obscure; this is because we become aware during the work of interpretation that at that point there is a tangle of dream-thoughts which cannot be unravelled and which moreover adds nothing to our knowledge of the content of the dream. This is the dream's navel, the spot where it reaches down into the unknown. (*SE* 5, p. 525)

Dreams end up blocking the very interpretations they solicit. The paradox of interpretation is that it's complete only when it runs up against the impossibility of completion. The frustration of tugging at knots that can't be unravelled is the counterintuitive signal that we've learned something about the dream. In our present dream, this frustration sets in at the approach to the strange word *tutelrein*. Let's follow Freud's division of the word into its two component parts.

The word *tutel* condenses a number of contradictory associations. It is, said Freud, 'a legal term for "guardianship" [tutelage]', connoting a rather formalized, legalistic conception of parental authority. And yet it is, 'also a vulgar term for a woman's breast' – in our own idiom, a tit. An ambiguity immediately asserts itself – *tutel* expresses simultaneously the empty form and the dense content of the parent–child relationship, both anonymous paternal authority and loving maternal care. For the child, *tutel* signifies the external 'tutelary' discipline to which he must submit, and the internal desire for the breast he can't control. That the word is at once formal and vulgar only intensifies this ambiguity, intimating an affinity between parental authority and erotic desire – 'guardian' and 'tit'; discipline and transgression blend into one another.

The condensation of meanings multiplies further when *tutel* is brought into contact with *rein*. The compound *tutelrein* suggests both, 'free of guardianship/higher authority' and 'free of the tit' – that is, a mature, self-regulating adult, 'weaned' from maternal desire and dependency. But Freud suggests that this adult autonomy or 'cleanliness' is haunted by its opposite, bringing *rein* into association with the first half of 'Zimmertelegraph' (house-telephone) to form *zimmerrein* (house-trained), 'closely connected with making the floor wet'. In this way, the wetting and continuous ringing of the *Zimmertelegraph* becomes the nodal point for conflicting ideas of the adult and the infantile, discipline and desire, continence and incontinence. Doesn't the repairman's pronouncement allude to this internal conflict?: 'It's a funny thing that even people who are "tutelrein" as a rule are quite unable to deal with a thing like this.'

One way of translating the repairman's statement is: 'it's funny that people who think they're beyond infantile desires are in fact still in their grip'. For if the overturned glass of water is brought into association with *zimmerrein*, it suggests bed-wetting, the boy's primary manifestation of what Freud terms 'urethral eroticism'. A boy's incontinence is an index not of weakness but of his unconscious sexual ambition and aggression. No wonder it wakes his father. This masculine rivalry in turn evokes the *tutel* once more, the boy's desire to possess the mother's tit and the 'drops' that 'fall' from it. Yet the same rivalry at once recalls the *tutel*age of his father, which separates him from the desired breast. These infantile images, to complicate matters further, may be overlaid by later adolescent ones – the falling drops of milk and urine succeeded by falling drops of sperm. Under cover of night, whilst his father is sleeping, the adolescent boy takes the opportunity to give vent to the desires a self-possessed young man is enjoined to master. And to cap it all, the *zimmerrein* that signals all this wetting echoes the name of a (guiltily desired?) family member.

This elaboration of Freud's interpretation emphatically does not, we should note in passing, unravel 'the tangle of dream thoughts' at the dream's navel. In drawing out its possible meanings, we neither resolve nor explain it, but simply reveal the unknowable and excessive sources from which it might emerge.

Tutelrein is thus abundant with condensations. It reveals the indelible imprint the suckling baby, the bed-wetting child and the masturbating adolescent have left on the psyche of the man. It also brings alive the ongoing struggle between punishing self-discipline and unregulated desire that haunts the life of the mind. The dream enables these incompatible claims to, citing the previous extract once more, 'form an intermediate aim, a compromise'. It's no accident that such compromises are formed verbally, for, 'words, since they are the nodal points of numerous ideas, may be regarded as predestined to ambiguity' (*SE* 5, p. 340).

Ambiguity has many uses, the most basic of which is defensive. As Emma's symptoms showed us, it enables the intolerable truth to assume the guise of the innocuously trivial. What Freud called the 'superficial' interrelation of images in the dream by means of 'assonance, verbal ambiguity . . . or any association of the kind we allow in jokes or in play upon words' is the index of, 'a deeper link between them which is subjected to the resistance of the censorship' (*SE* 5, p. 530). Joking, in other words, is deadly serious: like poetry, it diverts attention from *sense*, reference to an external world to *sound*, the sonic and rhythmic properties of words themselves. Witty words serve themselves rather than the world beyond them.

It's this logic of diversion that makes the joke such a rich resource for the dream, providing the latter with a language for simultaneously expressing and concealing what it wishes to say. Jokes and dreams make audible the ambiguity we conventionally silence in order to make ourselves intelligible – everyday life can't be efficiently conducted in puns. 'In waking reality I have little claim to be regarded as a wit', wrote Freud in his footnote. Wit, by introducing duplicity into communication, compromises the clarity and intelligibility to which the man of science is responsible. Thankfully for both himself and the history of modern thought, 'the peculiar psychological conditions under which dreams are constructed' give him the license to abandon this responsibility at night. Placing a block in the path of direct expression, dreams subject thoughts to a labyrinthine diversion that 'forces' them into being both obscure and curiously funny.

Dreams preserve at least a semblance of sense by subjecting unconscious thoughts to a rudimentary grammar and syntax. But if we attempt to communicate the wilfully contradictory contents of the unconscious without any such disguise, they can only cancel out sense altogether – as we're about to discover.

4

THE COMICAL UNCONSCIOUS

In what instances, then, will a joke appear before criticism as nonsense? Particularly when it makes use of the modes of thought which are usual in the unconscious but which are proscribed in conscious thought – faulty reasoning, in fact. For certain modes of thought proper to the unconscious have also been retained by the conscious – for instance some kinds of indirect representation, allusion, and so on – even though their conscious employment is subject to considerable restrictions. When a joke makes use of these techniques it will raise little or no objection on the part of criticism; objections will only appear if it also makes use for its technique of the methods with which conscious thought will have nothing more to do. A joke can still avoid objection, if it conceals the faulty reasoning it has used and disguises it under a show of logic [. . .]. But if it produces the faulty reasoning undisguised, then the objections of criticism will follow with certainty.

In such cases the joke has another resource. The faulty reasoning, which it uses for its technique as one of the modes of thought of the unconscious, strikes criticism – even though not invariably so – as being *comic*. Consciously giving free play to unconscious modes of thought (which have been rejected as faulty) is a means of producing comic pleasure; and it is easy to understand this, since it certainly requires a greater expenditure of energy to establish a preconscious cathexis than to give free play to an unconscious one. When, on hearing a thought which has, as it were, been formed in the unconscious, we compare it with its correction, a difference in expenditure emerges for us from which comic pleasure arises. A joke which makes use of faulty reasoning like this for its technique, and therefore appears nonsensical, can thus produce a comic effect at the same time. If we fail to detect the joke, we are once again left with only the comic or funny story.

The story of the borrowed kettle which had a hole in it when it was given back is an excellent example of the purely comic effect of giving free play to the unconscious mode of thought. It will be recalled that the borrower, when he was questioned, replied firstly that he had not borrowed a kettle at all, secondly that it had had a hole in it already when he borrowed it, and thirdly that he had given it back undamaged and without a hole. This mutual cancelling-out by several thoughts, each of which is in itself valid, is precisely what does not occur in the unconscious.

Extract from *Jokes and Their Relation to the Unconscious, SE* 8, pp. 204–5

Denied direct access to consciousness, the unconscious can make itself heard only by means of the most elaborate ruses. These ruses provoke laughter on account of their ingenious circumventions of the logical and syntactical laws governing conscious thinking. The unconscious is nothing if not resourceful: if its contents are refused expression in the form of 'a normal and serious association', it will make use instead of 'a superficial and apparently absurd one' (*SE* 5, p. 531). Nor, as Freud was surprised to find from his dream analyses, is the unconscious inhibited by pride in its choice of associative paths: 'No connection was too loose, no joke too bad, to serve as a bridge from one thought to another' (*SE* 5, p. 530). Like an excitable child (or low-grade celebrity), the unconscious will do anything to get our attention.

Our passage from Freud's 1905 book, *Jokes and Their Relation to the Unconscious* (*Der Witz und seine Beziehung zum Unbewussten*), makes this shamelessness peculiarly vivid. The absurdity of dream-thinking is redeemed in part by an admirable spirit of invention. The dream drafts into service a battery of verbal and sonic weapons: 'assonance, verbal ambiguity, temporal coincidence without connection in meaning, or any association of the kind we allow in jokes or in play on words' (*SE* 5, p. 530). In contrast, the 'comic' species of joke discussed here (exemplified by the 'borrowed kettle' joke), dispenses with these ingenious stratagems in favour of something simultaneously more impoverished and more guileful: sheer ineptitude. Comic reasoning doesn't bother disguising or compensating for the brazenly 'faulty reasoning' of unconscious thinking. On the contrary, it works by 'consciously giving free play to unconscious modes of thought'.

This conscious play of the unconscious points to an obvious and significant distinction between dreams and parapraxes on the one hand and jokes on the other. The wit of dreams and parapraxes is entirely unconscious. Freud avowedly had 'little claim to be regarded as a wit' in his waking life, but is made one – unwittingly – by his dreams. The joke, in contrast, is a space consciously designated by a culture for the expression of unconscious impulses. Like children, jokes are distinguished by a licence to violate logic and propriety which is denied to normative adult communication.

Nevertheless, for the joke as for the dream, this licence has its limits. Whilst jokes can take advantage of a relaxation of the laws of consistency and coherence that govern everyday reasoning, they are bound to maintain at least a semblance of submission to these laws. Take the example of the 'Salmon Mayonnaise' joke to which Freud returns repeatedly throughout *Der Witz*. An impoverished would-be gourmand borrows twenty-five florins from a wealthy acquaintance, who discovers his debtor in a restaurant the following day, with a plate of salmon mayonnaise before him. The lender reproaches him for using his money for this indulgence. The borrower replies, 'I don't understand you . . . if I haven't any money I *can't* eat salmon mayonnaise and if I have some money I *musn't* eat salmon mayonnaise. Well, then, when *am* I supposed to eat salmon mayonnaise?' (*SE* 8, p. 50).

This belongs to that class of jokes which Freud, in our chosen passage, describes as concealing 'faulty reasoning . . . under a show of logic'. Its appearance of logic is achieved by means of the now-familiar mechanism of displacement: the debtor diverts his acquaintance's grave demand as to why he's eating salmon *at all* to the trivial question of *when* he's to eat salmon. But the displacement is more than an amusing mechanism of obfuscation. As Freud argued, the joke works to disguise the vociferous demand of the pleasure principle, in all its sovereign indifference to reality. It gives distorted voice to the assertion, 'that the wishes and desires of men have the right to make themselves acceptable alongside of exacting and ruthless morality' (*SE* 8, p. 110).

Jokes provide a fleeting experience of a world in which this will to pleasure is given free reign. The laughter they generate punctures the inhibiting seriousness of the external world's demands. Enforcing this rule of seriousness is no light task; it involves a high degree of 'psychical expenditure' (*SE* 8, p. 118). The pleasure of the joke consists in the *saving* of this expenditure, in relief from the demand to uphold the inhibitions that sustain normative social and mental life. The impoverished gourmand's *chutzpah* provokes laughter because it inverts the hierarchy of reality over pleasure that governs everyday experience.

Of course, this inversion of values should be familiar to us from dreams, which are similarly impelled by the force of wishes, as well as the imperative, imposed by repression, to disguise and distort those wishes. In the young man's dream of the previous chapter, this disguise took the form above all of condensation: the word *tutel* condensed within itself both a repressed wish for the 'tit' and the repressing authority of 'tutelage'. The wish expressed in the salmon mayonnaise joke achieves its indirect fulfilment by means of displacement: the reproachful question, 'why are you eating salmon at all?' is diverted to the trivial question 'why are you eating salmon now?' It is on the basis of these shared mechanisms of distortion that Freud identifies a 'joke-work' correlative to the dream-work. In both cases, wishes have to work around their prohibition.

Nevertheless, this work involves a lower investment of mental energy than is required for conscious thought processes. This 'difference in expenditure' between joke thinking and normative thinking, says Freud, is the very source of the joke's pleasure. (There is, of course, an inverse and very large 'difference in expenditure' between telling and interpreting a joke. The mental labour involved in the latter may explain why conventional wisdom avers that nothing kills laughter so much as its analysis. On the other hand, isn't there something about the disproportion between the weight of theoretical speculation and the lightness of the joke that is itself funny?).

The creditor in the salmon mayonnaise joke demands that his beneficiary meet the exacting requirements of logic and morality, to which the latter effectively replies, 'But if that means I can't eat what I want, *I can't be bothered*'! Of course, this is the effective, not the actual response, and there's an important difference. The actual response is a piece of sophistry, a contemptuous parody of sound reasoning, whereas the effective response it disguises is an unconscious wish, in all its brazen indifference to the law of non-contradiction: 'I want money to stay afloat, and I want money to eat salmon mayonnaise.' This of course conflicts provocatively with the lender's insistence that the money is for one and not the other. In other words, to invoke terms from 'The Unconscious' once more: where the lender, speaking from the vantage-point of external reality (or consciousness), sees an 'either-or', the borrower, speaking from the vantage-point of psychical reality (or the unconscious), knows only a 'both-and'.

Now the borrower is pragmatic enough to know that this 'both-and' cannot be nakedly asserted, or 'given free play', without flagrantly and self-defeatingly affronting basic logic and morality, or what Freud in our passage called 'criticism'. His displacement of the lender's reproachful question is a way of circumventing such criticism and thereby of making us laugh.

But our passage raises another question: what if a joke dispenses with even this show of logic? What if instead it 'produces the faulty reasoning undisguised'? Another way of asking the question: can there be a joke *without joke-work*? Isn't laughter an effect of the ingenious displacements and condensations of joke-work? Without them, what is there to laugh at? Freud's immediate answer is, indeed, nothing: 'if it produces the faulty reasoning undisguised, then the objections of criticism will follow with certainty'. But this assertion is followed by an immediate qualification: the joke can evade these objections by passing itself off as *comic*.

The impoverished gourmet couldn't stretch to an *inhibitory* expenditure of mental energy: the mental expense of renunciation exceeded (in his own, not very objective, estimation), the financial expense of indulgence. But he at least gave his lender the minimal courtesy of a show of logic, trying to effect some compromise, however laughably unconvincing, between external and psychical reality. The borrower of the kettle, possessed entirely by his psychical reality, denies *his* lender even this much. Giving 'free play to the unconscious mode of thought', he denies first the act of borrowing, then his responsibility for its consequences, then the consequences themselves.

This self-incriminating sequence of excuses illuminates the unconscious process in at least two ways. First, it brings us tantalizingly close to the dense, formless reality of the unconscious, in which radically incompatible facts exist side by side, oblivious to one another's presence. But second, it demonstrates that the unconscious cannot survive its translation into the conscious intact. What is possible in psychical reality becomes impossible in external reality: 'This mutual cancelling-out by several thoughts, each of which is in itself valid, is precisely what does not occur in the unconscious.' For consciousness, a statement of fact can't coexist with its contradiction – or, you can't have your cake and eat it.

Freud more than once cited Kant's definition of the comic as, 'an expectation that has turned to nothing' (*SE* 8, p. 199). Kant is thinking of the double movement by which comedy raises and then defuses tension, but his description takes on a different resonance alongside the 'borrowed kettle' joke. For by saying too much – that is, by asserting facts radically incompatible with one another – the borrower says precisely *nothing*. Trying to render the unconscious process in conscious language is like exposing undeveloped camera film: the light of day erases the contents in each case.

In fact, this analogy is as faulty as it is neat. For where nothing of the image on the negative survives its exposure, something of the borrower's unconscious thoughts survive their expression. In the comic joke, the unconscious thought has a protective veneer that the undeveloped negative lacks: the veneer of the comic. The comic, according to Freud, seduces 'criticism' into relaxing its austere regime. King Lear, remember, won't hear objectionable sentiments from anyone but the Fool.

The difference between the salmon mayonnaise and the kettle jokes, then, is the difference between wit and the comic; the comic dispenses with the *work* wit makes so audible. In the kettle joke, there is no displacement or condensation, no sonic, rhythmic or semantic wordplay, nothing but the raw and undisguised contradictions of the unconscious. This raises an obvious question: how is the comic allowed to get away with such shameless idleness? What is contained in the formula of the comic veneer that distracts criticism from its task?

I'm going to call upon Hans Christian Andersen's tale of 'The Emperor's New Clothes'[6] to help shed light on this question. The tale's two rogues, recall, are commissioned by the dandyish Emperor to weave the beautiful clothes they claim will be invisible to anyone unfit for the office they hold. Affecting to work busily on their looms, the rogues in fact do nothing at all. The emissaries sent by the Emperor to inspect the work in progress duly detect nothing on the looms, but are inhibited from saying so for fear of exposing their unfitness for office. Thus it is that the Emperor himself is eventually cajoled into declaring the magnificence of the non-existent clothes, and into donning them for a procession through his capital's streets. The members of the gathered crowd, each fearful of revealing his own stupidity, collude in the enforcement of this now collective delusion, which is finally punctured by a small child exclaiming: 'But the Emperor has nothing on at all!' (Andersen 1992, p. 109).

What happens if we read the Emperor's love of elaborate disguise as a figure for the love of wit? After all, wit, as we've seen, requires a good deal of elaborate weaving – the warp of displacement, the woof of condensation. Andersen's rogues, however, whilst affecting to weave in fact do nothing, and this nothing finally manifests itself in the nakedness of the Emperor. Doesn't the behaviour of the Court and the public before their naked sovereign curiously resemble the behaviour of 'criticism' before the comic? Both parties are held back as if spellbound from objecting to a brazen violation of the logic of external reality. But by what? By the illusion woven by the rogues and the comic alike. The comic behaves like Andersen's rogues in the sense that he manages to persuade its audience that the unconscious impulse's nakedness is concealed. But, just as all that is concealing the Emperor is the collective delusion of his subjects, so all that is concealing the unconscious thought is the spell woven by the comic itself. Something in the undisguised shamelessness of the kettle's borrower, as in the spectacular audacity of the rogues, blunts the edge of criticism's knife. Of course, only a child's fearless indifference to the reality principle (ironically, it is fear of the punishment which reality will inflict upon the 'stupid' and 'unfit' that sustains the pervasive *un*reality) sharpens the critic once more.

Wit and the comic are distinguished, then, by the different relationships they forge between psychical and external reality. Wit, recognising the demands of each, tries to broker a compromise between them: the question, 'when *am* I supposed to eat salmon mayonnaise?' is the piece of displaced external reality with which the borrower conceals the ravenous claim of his psychical reality. The comic, on the other hand, at least as manifested in the kettle joke, involves a wholesale refusal of external reality. Confronted with the hole he put in the kettle, the borrower chooses withdrawal into the madness of internal reality over acknowledgement of the external fact. As 'The Emperor's New Clothes' so vividly shows, external reality is in this respect shockingly vulnerable to the sudden and unyielding demands of its psychical counterpart. Indeed, literature is replete with illustrations of this vulnerability: think of Hermia's traumatized reaction to the collapse of her external reality in *A Midsummer Night's Dream*. Within minutes of being told by her previously tender lover that he hates her and loves her best friend, she is reduced to doubting the very self that separates inside from outside, a separation without which sanity dissolves: 'Am I not Hermia?' (Act III, Sc. 2).

Wit, it would seem, is distinguished from the comic in just the way that, for Freud, neurosis is distinguished from psychosis. Wit resembles neurosis in that its creations, like neurotic symptoms, simultaneously express unconscious impulses and their repression: Emma's phobia made visible both her repressed sexual desires and the repressive fears attaching to them. The comic, in contrast, brings us closer to psychosis. 'In neurosis', Freud wrote in his 1924 essay, 'The Loss of Reality in Neurosis and Psychosis', 'a piece of reality is avoided by a sort of flight' (*SE* 19, p. 185). The point here is that this flight is nevertheless an acknowledgement of the unwanted reality. Psychosis, in contrast, disavows the reality it doesn't wish to confront – denies its existence, just as the borrower denies the hole he made, and the Court denies the emperor's nakedness.

This may explain why the kettle joke is more uncomfortable than funny – the same reason, in fact, that Hermia's horrified question, spoken properly, can insinuate an eerie break in the audience's laughter. It may conversely explain why 'mad people', against our better judgement, tempt us to nervous laughter. Of course, even in the comic, and even in psychosis, the unconscious assumes disguises: but these disguises are transparent, and the glimpse they afford of the unconscious in all its formless chaos leaves us unsure whether to laugh or cry.

5

NO

The manner in which our patients bring forward their associations during the work of analysis gives us an opportunity for making some interesting observations. 'Now you'll think I mean to say something insulting, but really I've no such intention.' We realize that this is a rejection, by projection, of an idea that has just come up. Or: 'You ask who this person in the dream can be. It's *not* my mother.' We emend this to 'So it *is* my mother.' In our interpretation, we take the liberty of disregarding the negation and picking out the subject-matter alone of the association. It is as though the patient had said: 'It's true that my mother came into my mind as I thought of this person, but I don't feel inclined to let the association count.'

There is a very convenient method by which we can sometimes obtain a piece of information about unconscious repressed material. 'What', we ask, 'would you consider the most unlikely imaginable thing in that situation? What do you think was furthest from your mind at that time?' If the patient falls into the trap and says what he thinks is most incredible, he almost always makes the right admission. [. . .]

Thus the content of a repressed image or idea can make its

way into consciousness, on condition that it is *negated*. Negation
is a way of taking cognizance of what is repressed; indeed it is
already a lifting of the repression, though not, of course, an
acceptance of what is repressed.

Extract from 'Negation', SE 19, pp. 235–6

The mechanism of negation (*Verneinung*), like that of dis-
avowal (*Verleugnung*) involves the denial (in fact a more
common translation of *Verneinung*) of a seemingly self-evident
piece of reality. Negation, as Freud argues in his highly compressed essay of 1925, is the mind's judgement of an object as
unreal. It belongs, Freud notes, to the drive he had identified
in *Beyond the Pleasure Principle* five years earlier, as 'destructive'.
The destructive or 'death-drive' (which we'll treat much more
extensively in Chapter Nine) is the human organism's will to
'defusion' or disintegration, in opposition to the integrative
and unifying drives to life and love. Little wonder, then, that
'the general wish to negate' is particularly prominent 'in some
psychotics' (*SE* 19, p. 239).

Our concern in this chapter isn't with the mechanism of
negation as such, but with its specific appearance in the setting
of psychoanalytic treatment: that is, with the patient's rejection of her own thought as unreal. Freud's implication is that
rejections of this kind attest to a kernel of latent psychosis in
each of us, which denies whatever in reality it finds intolerable. For the analyst, the patient's negation of a thought clears
a path to the truth of her unconscious, for what her 'no'
really registers is a thought too painfully alien to acknowledge.

The journey from the patient's mouth to the analyst's ear
thus turns her 'no' into a 'yes', and affords him access to her
deepest secrets. Our passage points to just why Freud and
psychoanalysis have never ceased to provoke intense suspicion

and exasperation. Doesn't the first paragraph betray an insidious authoritarianism? If the patient insists the figure in the dream is not his mother, 'we emend [*berichtigen* – literally "correct", "put right"] this to: "So it *is* his mother."' More than one reader, and indeed more than one patient might be tempted at this point to demand angrily of Freud, just who are *you* to emend what *I've* said? Who are you to rob me of that most precious right to define the meaning of what I say and do, of my authority over, my *authorship of* my own words?

Let's push this angry response a little further by means of the underhand tactic of pitting these against other sentences in the Freudian corpus. Freud, we might observe caustically, was so busy alerting his patients to their psychotic tendencies that he seems not to notice his own. After all, he himself had written of paranoiacs three years previously that, 'they let themselves be guided by their knowledge of the unconscious, and displace to the unconscious minds of others the attention which they have withdrawn from their own.' (*SE* 18, p. 226). Doesn't this description uncannily approximate the analyst's righting of the patient's verbal wrongs? He too harnesses the knowledge of his unconscious to penetrate into another's, revealing its secret meanings with the certainty of the seer. Notice how, like a good paranoiac, he sets 'traps' he knows the patient will fall into.

There's something to this protest, and we'll try to indicate in due course just what it is. But it's also flawed by its unquestioning assumption of the very integrity and transparency of the self that psychoanalysis puts in question. To object that I know the meaning of my thoughts and feelings better than the analyst is rather too conveniently to forget that I came to analysis in the first place because I had in some way or another

become *strange* to myself. People came to Freud, as they continue to come to analysts today, for many different reasons:
they were experiencing unaccountable phobic reactions; or
they were suffering physical symptoms – vomiting, stuttering,
phantom smells, partial paralyses – which eluded medical
diagnosis; or they were compelled to perform actions and rit-
uals whose meanings and motivations were tormentingly
obscure to them; or, more straightforwardly, they were miser-
able, for reasons they understood either inadequately or not at
all. But what recurs across these very different motivations is
the sense that some unrecognisable and incomprehensible
force is struggling to make itself present to the conscious
mind. Put another way, some physical dysfunction or emotional impasse is registering with peculiar and painful clarity
that, as the poet Arthur Rimbaud famously wrote, '"I" is an
other' (*'"Je" est un autre'*). I come to analysis because when I
say, 'I', I don't know, or no longer know, just who or what I
am, or indeed 'I' is.

Free association, repeatedly designated by Freud the 'fundamental rule' of psychoanalytic treatment, is the slow and
laborious method by which the patient experiences and
comes to terms with this radical self-alienation. Lying on her
back, unencumbered by the inhibiting distractions of the analyst (who sits behind her) and his visible reactions, the patient
is enjoined to say whatever comes to mind, however trivial,
false, unpleasant or incoherent it may sound to her own ears.
By faithful adherence to this rule, the patient is led falteringly
to the unconscious sources of her symptoms.

We should be aware by now, however, that the path
between the patient's words and their unconscious meanings
is far from straight. Even for the most conscientious followers
of the 'fundamental rule', the path is beset from beginning to

end by unforeseen obstacles and forced diversions. One of the many paradoxes of free association is that it can be most revealing when least free, that is, when the patient *resists*, consciously or not, the passage of her own insight. This paradox may provide our first, tentative clue as to why Freud was unwilling to take at face value a protestation such as 'It's *not* my mother'. An unconscious thought may be revealed in and by the patient's very act of censoring, dismissing or overruling it: 'Negation is a way of taking cognizance of what is repressed.' Resistances simultaneously block and clear the passage to unconscious truth. Indeed, Freud seems to suggest in this extract, they themselves are the means by which the unconscious transmits its concealed contents. It is these transmissions, carried on a frequency outside the range of normal human listening and frequently drowned out by the white noise of resistance, to which the analyst must attune the ear of his own unconscious, 'as a telephone receiver is adjusted to the transmitting microphone' (*SE* 12, p. 115).

Negation, then, must take its place alongside neurotic symptoms, parapraxes, and the displacements and condensations of dreams and jokes, in the repertory of disguises by which the unconscious simultaneously conceals and exposes itself. It provides further attestation to the fragility of my claim to control the meaning of my words and actions, especially in the analytic setting. As Freud puts it in 'The Unconscious': 'all the acts and manifestations which I notice in myself and do not know how to link up with the rest of my mental life must be judged as if they belonged to someone else: they are to be explained by a mental life ascribed to this person' (*SE* 14, p. 169). Analysis begins from the startling insight that when 'I' speak, I am simultaneously and unknowingly ventriloquizing this someone else, someone both radically distant from and tantalizingly close to me. It is this 'someone else' that goes by the name of the unconscious.

From his early work with hysterics onward, Freud was concerned with the different possible consequences of refusing to acknowledge this 'someone else'. The unconscious, he found, doesn't take kindly to being ignored. We can more clearly illuminate this tendency to vindictiveness by casting it in the light of Freud's second model of the mind as laid out in *The Ego and the Id*. He posits here that the mind is originally nothing more than a formless repository of erotic and destructive drives, or *id* (*Es*, literally 'it'). Mental development consists in the formation of a 'coherent organization of mental processes' (*SE* 19, p. 17) at the surface of the *id*, which controls all those functions associated with the conscious, purposive self, and which is on that account termed by Freud the *Ich* – the I, or in Strachey's now well-established translation, the ego. The ego, in other words, is the settler in a place where the *id*'s aboriginal; little wonder the latter is resentful when cast out and ignored by its usurper. Evicted from a portion of its own territory, it comes back to stake its claim, to remind its tenant who first occupied the land.

And there is worse to come for the beleaguered ego, for if it's fighting a grass-roots rebellion from the unconscious *id* below, it's also set upon by an authoritarian force, equally unconscious and thereby equally fearsome, above. As we learnt in Chapter One, my earliest libidinal drives are doomed to frustration by the prohibition imposed upon them. This prohibition is embodied above all in the figure of my father, who dislodges me traumatically from the privileged position of lover to my mother. This drama of desire and its prohibition, known of course as the Oedipus complex, is implanted deep in my unconscious memory, from which it emits periodic punishing reminders of its presence in the form of a message: 'You *may not be* like this (like your father) – that is, you may not do all that he does; some things are his prerogative' (*SE* 19, p. 34). The speaker of this forbidding message goes by the name of the super-ego, or *Über-Ich*.

Why this diversion into Freud's second topology of the mind? Perhaps to show just how monstrously ambiguous is the 'someone else' within me. It (he? she?) speaks in the rapacious voice of aimless desire at one moment, and in the wrathful voice of patrician authority at the next. Who would want to know this someone else? Who would not be prone to respond to the sight of such a fearsome and capriciously changeable being with the words, 'no, I'm sorry, I don't know you'. Or, 'It's *not* my mother.'

To this insistence that I don't know this someone else, the analyst can only respond with gentle insistence that yes, you do (or yes, 'I' does). 'I' protests angrily, 'this is *my* house, I built it, I paid for it, and I won't have squatters claiming rights here!' 'I' would rather forget that it built on someone else's land and even used their materials; the ego is only an organised portion of, a little pocket of fragile coherence within the *id*.

Freud knew just how devastating a revelation this was. In more than one place, he characterises it as the third in a three-fold blow dealt by science across the centuries to humankind's confident self-image. The first of these was the Copernican displacement of the earth from the centre to the outermost margins of the cosmos. The second was Darwin's demonstration of the descent of the human from the animal kingdom. But, he continues, 'human megalomania will have suffered its third and most wounding blow from the psychological research of the present time which seeks to prove to the ego that it is *not even master in its own house* [my emphasis], but must content itself with scanty information of what is going on unconsciously in its mind' (*SE* 16, p. 285).

It's no doubt possible to get through life without feeling this blow, without paying much mind to the someone else speaking through my slips, dreams, fantasies and anxieties. But it's also possible to be sufficiently compelled by the fear, unhappiness, confusion or even sheer curiosity induced by the nagging presence of this someone else to seek an analyst. And by means of this odd pairing, forged in the simple agreement of the one to talk and the other to listen, the hazy, shapeless outline of this someone else comes slowly into focus.

Negation, like all resistances, expresses the ego's persistent preference to turn and run from this someone else when it approaches too closely. The analyst's task is to find a way to hold the ego to the spot, to persuade it to follow the unconscious rather than give it the slip. Put another way, the analyst encourages his patient to maintain the freedom of her associations in the face of her ego's tyrannizing fear of that freedom. Negation is an expression of this fear, an attempt to put a brake on the exhilaratingly bumpy ride toward someone else. The authoritarian tone of Freud's 'So it *is* my mother' must be heard as a counter-move against the authoritarianism the patient exercises against herself. His rewording of the patient's negation as, 'I don't feel inclined to let the association count' vividly illuminates this will to self-censorship, the imposition of a limit on freedom of association. The ego's negations defend against the intolerably unrecognisable double which seems at times to speak through it, the someone else who'd dare to insult the revered analyst or dream about mother.

Freud insisted, then, on the importance of listening to negations for what they might intimate in spite of their own intentions. If the patient uses her 'no' to pull a thought out of the chain of association, the analyst must use the same 'no' to thread it back in. This conception of resistance as means rather than obstacle to truth was central to the psychoanalytic enterprise from the beginning.

Witnessing the hypnotic demonstrations of the renowned Hippolyte Bernheim in 1889 had helped persuade Freud of the incontestable existence of the unconscious. And yet he was as disturbed by Bernheim's coercive treatment of his subjects as he was impressed by the results. He recalled that 'when a patient who showed himself unamenable was met with the shout: 'What are you doing? *Vous vous contre-suggestionez!*', I said to myself that this was an evident injustice and an act of violence' (*SE* 18, p. 89). For Bernheim, resistance was a nuisance, an unaccountable compulsion to stand in the way of one's own cure. Unlike Freud, Bernheim took the patient's resistance at face value – his 'no' means 'no'. But it was just this quickness to take the patient at his word that betrayed his real authoritarianism; Bernheim's 'act of violence' consisted in his inability to experience the subject's resistance as anything other than an impudent obstruction of his purposes. Conversely, Freud's intense receptivity to resistance grounds interpretation in a principle other than the tyrannical one of whether the patient says what he expects to hear. In his 'Recommendations to Physicians on Psycho-Analytic Technique', he wrote: 'In making his selection, if he [the analyst] follows his expectations he is in danger of never finding anything but what he already knows' (*SE* 12, p. 112). Psychoanalytic listening can be described as a striving to receive from the patient what neither she nor the analyst 'already knows', the unexpected and unrecognisable desires of the someone else concealed behind 'my' words.

This someone else speaks a strange language – the 'timeless' language of the unconscious, foreign to the definitive clarity of opposing terms. 'We never', wrote Freud at the end of 'Negation', 'discover a "no" in the unconscious' (*SE* 19, p. 239). Nor, for that matter, could we discover a 'yes', inasmuch as the one term derives its meaning from its opposition to the other. We discover in the unconscious a language that resembles more the poetic speech to which the great German-language poet Paul Celan enjoins the reader in his 'Speak, You Also': 'Speak – / But keep yes and no unsplit./ And give your say this meaning: / give it the shade.'[7]

Negation, in which a 'yes' is silently intimated by way of a 'no', partakes of just such 'shady' meaning. And if Freud's thinking rings in any way false in this passage, it may be because it doesn't sufficiently respect this shadiness. In 'taking the liberty of disregarding the negation', in countering the rigid certainty of the patient's 'no' with the inverse certainty of his 'yes', he betrayed his own insight into the ineradicable ambiguity of speech, and especially analytic speech.

In 'Constructions in Analysis' a very late and very rich paper from 1937, Freud recognised the need to be more equivocal towards the patient's 'no': 'a patient's 'No' is no evidence of the correctness of a construction . . . the only safe interpretation of his 'No' is that it points to incompleteness' (*SE* 23, p. 263). The patient's 'no' registers the haunting presence of the someone else, who deprives the speaking 'I' of his cherished authority over his words. This someone else speaks from the unhomely position of incompleteness, beyond the reassuring certainties of yes and no.

6

DOUBLY UNCANNY

At this point I will put forward two considerations which, I think, contain the gist of this short study. In the first place, if the psycho-analytic study is correct in maintaining that every affect belonging to an emotional impulse, whatever its kind, is transformed, if it is repressed, into anxiety, then among instances of frightening things there must be one class in which the frightening element can be shown to be something repressed which *recurs*. This class of frightening things would then constitute the uncanny; and it must be a matter of indifference whether what is uncanny is itself originally frightening or whether it carried some *other* affect. In the second place, if this is indeed the secret nature of the uncanny, we can understand why linguistic usage has extended *das Heimliche* [homely] into its opposite, *das Unheimliche*; for this uncanny is in reality nothing new or alien, but something which is familiar and old-established in the mind and which has become alienated from it only through the process of repression. This reference to the factor of repression enables us, furthermore, to understand Schelling's definition of the uncanny as something which ought to have remained hidden but has come to light.

Extract from 'The Uncanny', *SE* 17, p. 241

Negation is a resistance to the revelation of oneself as more than one self. It is directed against the unrecognisable double or 'someone else' who seems at times to take possession of my voice. The essay from which our present passage is extracted is an extended meditation on the unnerving or *uncanny* feeling induced by this double.

A negation paradoxically acknowledges a thought or feeling by disowning it. Freud's attention had been drawn to this singular state of mind at least as early as 1892, when he treated the English governess 'Miss Lucy R.', the third of the five case histories collected in *Studies on Hysteria*. Lucy R. was relieved of her hysterical symptom, an insistent smell of burnt pudding, by recalling the repressed impulse – the unrequited love of her employer – the smell displaces. Lucy R. so casually admitted this love when Freud put it to her that he asked in surprise, 'But if you knew you loved your employer why didn't you tell me?' Lucy R.'s short reply, in all its eloquent simplicity, is a canonical text of psychoanalytic history: 'I didn't know – or rather I didn't want to know' (*SE* 2, p. 117). The symptoms of hysteria, and indeed of all neuroses, take root in precisely this condition of doubleness. In the case of hysteria, the impulse the hysteric doesn't want to know is forced to make itself known by means of physical disguise or, in Freud's terminology, somatic *conversion*.

The enigma of the origin of the hysterical symptom is intensified in the Lucy R. case by the olfactory disguise of her repressed impulse. Smell is, of all the senses, the most intimately bound to its source: anyone can affirm the difficulty of dissociating the memory of a smell from the body, place or object specific to it. A smell has a *home*, and it's no accident that this truth is absorbed by so many of us in our childhood kitchens. Followed by the smell of burnt pudding, Lucy R.

experienced this truth negatively. The smell has severed itself
from the time and place that made it so potently meaningful,
the moment at which she both knew and didn't want to
know the depth of her feelings for her employer and his
family. The smell is the strange somatic residue of this internal conflict between knowing and its negation. If repression
has tamed the emotional fire, the burnt pudding attests that it
continues to smoke nonetheless. But Lucy R. didn't (want to)
know where the fire was. The smoke seems disturbingly out
of place or, to invoke the literal translation of Freud's famous
essay, unhomely (*Unheimlich*). Its unrecognizable strangeness
conceals an all too intimate familiarity.

Our passage identifies this paradox as the second of the
'two considerations which . . . contain the gist of this short
study': 'this uncanny is in reality nothing new or alien but
something which is familiar and old-established in the mind
and which has become alienated from it only through the
process of repression'. When an impulse driven into the
unconscious by repression reappears, it does so in the guise of
the uncanny. Repression puts distance between the mind and
a knowledge that has become intolerably intimate (rather like
an insistent bad smell). It is precisely this lost intimacy that
renders the return of this knowledge to the mind so eerie.
Strangeness is not the opposite, but the paradoxical *expression*
of intimacy, a point underlined by Freud's philological
unearthing of the word *Unheimlich* as originally an extension,
rather than a simple negation, of the *Heimlich*: 'we can understand why linguistic usage has extended *das Heimlich* into its
opposite'. The most familiar can be experienced after its
repression only in the form of the most alien: 'the frightening
element can be shown to be something repressed which
recurs'.

Doesn't this mean that, at least as far as psychoanalysis is concerned, there's a profound affinity between the uncanny and love? For love, defined by Freud as the infinitely complex ways in which the sexual drives of the body are played out in the mind, is the first and last motive for the force of repression: the very thing we know and don't want to know. It's for this reason that Lucy R.'s repressed love returned to her in such an uncanny form. Love is the most basic and inescapable way in which I (re)appear to myself as uncanny.

Freud focused his essay on the more typical associations of the uncanny, its morbidity and strangeness as manifested especially in the Gothic aesthetic of writers such as Edgar Allen Poe and Freud's own example of E. T. A. Hoffmann. And yet the essay also shows us persistently, if perhaps inadvertently, how the uncanny refuses to be localized in this way or to be reduced to a specific aesthetic sensibility. On the contrary, Freud assimilated to the uncanny all those primitive phenomena revealed by his own writings to persist in the 'civilized' mind – 'animism, magic and sorcery, the omnipotence of thoughts, man's attitude to death, involuntary repetition and the castration complex' (*SE* 17, p. 243). Nor was Freud slow to see where this line of thinking ultimately leads. Noting the Middle Ages' 'almost correct' ascription of madness to 'the influence of demons', he remarked: 'Indeed, I should not be surprised to hear that psychoanalysis, which is concerned with laying bare these hidden forces, has itself become uncanny for that very reason' (*SE* 17, p. 243).

The 'hidden forces' that bind psychoanalysis and the uncanny to one another are drives, both erotic and destructive, and, in the chapters to come, we'll discover what these involve. From the moment of birth, we are given over at once to love and to death, to a drive to expand and a drive to extinguish ourselves. These drives unconsciously assert their presence in an infinite variety of guises: phobic reactions to entering shops alone, inadvertently lewd puns, dreams of incontinently ringing telephones, pseudo-logical or downright illogical jokes, smells of burnt pudding. But in each of these cases, the unconscious represents me to myself as 'someone else', someone stubbornly unrecognizable. The unconscious is uncanny; and indeed, the Scottish etymology of 'canny', a derivative of 'ken', knowing (*kennen* in German), highlights the deep affinity of the two English terms. The 'hidden forces' within me destine me to be forever other to myself, to an indelible strangeness within.

As that which reveals this internal otherness, Freud seems to imply, psychoanalysis offers much more than a theory of the uncanny (as if theory could escape contamination by what it theorizes): it is *thinking itself become uncanny*. Psychoanalysis not only tells us about, in the philosopher Friedrich Schelling's definition, 'something which ought to have remained hidden but has come to light', it *is* such a 'something' itself.

A large portion of Freud's essay turns on a reading of Hoffmann's tale of 'The Sand-Man'. This reading affords him the opportunity both to demonstrate literature's unconscious use of key psychoanalytic motifs, and to affirm the uncanny undertow of those motifs. Most significant of these for Freud is the displaced castration anxiety he uncovers in the threat of the monstrous 'Sand-Man' (disguised as the lawyer Coppelius) to rob the young protagonist Nathaniel of his eyes: 'anxiety about one's eyes, the fear of going blind, is often enough a substitute for the fear of being castrated' (*SE* 17, p. 231).

The premise of the Oedipus complex is deceptively easy to summarize (and was already broached in the previous chapter): the child's recognition, around their fourth year, of their (his or her) father as rightful lover of their mother dislodges them traumatically from their own, phantasized occupation of this role. The father's power to effect this traumatizing recognition derives from the child's attendant phantasy that his prohibition of incest will be enforced by the punishment of castration. In the boy, this phantasy expresses itself as, 'I must renounce my desire to take father's place, or he'll castrate me.' In the girl, its form is: 'I realize that (like mother) I'm already castrated, and so must renounce my desire to take father's place.'

Though straightforward to define, complications arise in the *implausibility* of any such summary explanation. Ripped from the intricate texture of the everyday psychodynamics of childhood, or indeed from its painstaking reconstruction in the analyst's consulting room, an unmistakable arbitrariness, even absurdity, attaches to it. Why would anyone believe a story so brazenly fantastic? But in the context of a discussion of the uncanny, this absurdity is instructive: it brings home our radical and insuperable alienation from the inner life of the child we once were. If psychoanalysis is uncanny, it's because it once more makes visible this inner life, in the defamiliarizing but inextinguishable light of adult language and perception. 'I will show you', promised Freud at the outset of his course of *Introductory Lectures on Psycho-Analysis*, 'how the whole trend of your previous education and all your habits of thought are inevitably bound to make you into opponents of psycho-analysis' (*SE* 15, p. 15). Our 'previous education' and 'habits of thought' are geared towards the social, cultural and psychological repression of the 'hidden forces' which shape us from birth. Such an education can only prejudice its subjects against psychoanalysis and its uncanny revelations.

As the phantasy which shapes the child's first understanding of both desire and its prohibition, castration is perhaps the uncanniest of these revelations, a 'knowledge' with which children live in fearsome intimacy. Repression estranges this knowledge, rendering *unheimlich* what was once *heimlich*.

All of this, of course, has direct bearing on Freud's reading of the 'The Sand-Man', and especially on our pleasure and willingness to believe in such unlikely stories. What endows Hoffmann's story with such compelling power, he argued, is the symbolism of blinding, by means of which an intolerable knowledge breaks through its repression and returns to consciousness, albeit in distorted and alienated form. Under Freud's gaze, literature became a repository of displaced psychoanalytic knowledge, of the symbolic reinvention of our indelible childhood phantasies.

But as Nicholas Royle pointed out in his excellent study *The Uncanny*, there is a certain brutal instrumentality about this approach. Freud read 'The Sand-Man' by occluding its dense and subtle literary texture, by marginalizing or ignoring whatever in it fails to provide immediate illustrative support for his theoretical theses. He says nothing, Royle remarks, about the story's complex narrative structure, its use of the epistolary form, or the ingenious mirroring of the narrative's uncanny presentiments in the minds of the characters. In treating 'The Sand-Man' as evidence for his thesis of the uncanny, Freud does away with much of its uncanniness. But then, Freud is no more immune than anyone else to the impulse to resist the uncanny force of his own insights.

I want to end this chapter by way of a different approach to a different exemplar of the uncanny. Given that it too turns on the figures of blindness and insight, there's no doubt scope for interpretation along the same lines as Freud's reading of 'The

Sand-Man'. But I turn to Nathaniel Hawthorne's extraordinary story written in 1835, 'The Minister's Black Veil'[8] because I think its significance in this context is more than illustrative. Hawthorne's story isn't simply one among many instances of the literary uncanny, nor does it merely play out one or other psychoanalytic scenarios. It is a narrative meditation on the uncanny otherness at the heart of every human being, on the stubborn inextricability of the uncanny and the human. Indeed, it confirms Freud's essay in one key respect: the uncanniness it represents is entirely psychological, rather than supernatural, in origin. It tells of how an inanimate object comes to be endowed with an eerie and ominous inner life by all who look upon it.

Hawthorne's story begins with the sudden and unannounced decision of Reverend Hooper (based on an historical figure), minister of the New England town of Milford, to conceal his face permanently with a veil of folded black crape. The effect of this gesture on his congregants is immediate and dramatic. The minister's veiled face seems to cast a long shadow over the town and the inner life of its citizens: 'He has changed himself into something awful, only by hiding his face' (p. 98), remarks an old woman. The minister's sermon on 'secret sin' is felt as not only speaking about but somehow *enacting* its own theme: 'Each member of the congregation . . . felt as if the preacher had crept upon them, behind his awful veil, and discovered their hoarded iniquity of deed or thought' (p. 99). A melancholy pall spreads everywhere the minister appears, even at the wedding of Milford's 'handsomest couple' (p. 100).

Moreover, the veil seems to place a mysterious yet insuperable obstacle in the way of his congregants' attempts to question its meaning, as if portending 'a fearful secret between him and them' (p. 102). Even his wife's open-hearted and fearless attempt to cajole him into removing and disclosing the secret of the veil is met by a reiteration of his vow never to remove it whilst alive. Condemning himself to willed separation from his fellow human beings, the minister continues assiduously to perform his clerical duties from behind his veil.

In the story's climactic deathbed scene, the minister finally confesses the veil's meaning:

> What, but the mystery which it obscurely typifies, has made this piece of crape so awful? When the friend shows his inmost heart to his friend; the lover to his best-beloved; when man does not vainly shrink from the eye of his Creator, loathsomely treasuring up the secret of his sin; then deem me a monster, for the symbol beneath which I have lived, and die! I look around me, and, lo! on every visage, a Black Veil! (pp. 106–7)

What, then, is veiled by the veil? What fearsome secret does it conceal? The minister's final answer to the questions tormenting all those who face him is oddly tautological: my veil conceals a veil. Remove the black crape, and you won't find the unadorned Truth of my soul staring at you, but another layer of concealment, duplicity, doubleness. This uncanny truth, the minister teaches, is what our 'education' and 'habits of thought' induce us to forget. The veil is 'so awful' because it reminds us, not unlike psychoanalysis, that even without a veil we're in perpetual disguise, as obscure and unrecognizable to ourselves as to others. Indeed, the minister's sermon had gone so far as to make the startlingly proto-analytic point that we hide sin not only 'from our nearest and dearest' but equally 'from our own consciousness' (p. 99). We have estranged ourselves from our own most intimate knowledge, which, returned to us in the form of the minister's veil, can't but be darkly uncanny.

What the congregants are seeing in the veil, then, is nothing more than their own possession of an unconscious, their haunting by what Freud's essay calls a double of themselves: 'the quality of uncanniness can only come from the fact of the "double" being a creation dating back to a very early mental stage, long since surmounted' (*SE* 17, p. 236). 'Sin' perfectly captures the ambiguous essence of this double, for it alludes at once to the rapacious desires of the *id* and the censorious punishment of the superego. At once transgressive child and prohibitive parent, the unconscious double is itself double. The outward self or ego we present to the world enables us to pretend this double isn't there. My face, as I both know and don't want to know, is a black veil, disguising the uncanny other that 'I' is.

7

THE OBSCURE OBJECT OF DESIRE

THE SEXUAL OBJECT DURING EARLY INFANCY

But even after sexual activity has become detached from the taking of nourishment, an important part of this first and most significant of all sexual relations is left over, which helps to prepare for the choice of an object and thus to restore the happiness that has been lost. All through the period of latency children learn to feel for other people who help them in their helplessness and satisfy their needs a love which is on the model of, and a continuation of, their relation of sucklings to their nursing mother. There may perhaps be an inclination to dispute the possibility of identifying a child's affection and esteem for those who look after him with sexual love. I think, however, that a closer psychological examination may make it possible to establish this identity beyond any doubt. A child's intercourse with anyone responsible for his care affords him an unending source of sexual excitation and satisfaction from his erotogenic zones. This is especially so since the person in charge of him, who, after all, is as a rule his mother, herself regards him with feelings that are derived from her own sexual life: she strokes him, kisses him, rocks him and quite clearly treats him as a substitute for a complete sexual object. A mother would probably be horrified if she were made aware that all her marks of affection were rousing her child's sexual drive and preparing for its later intensity. She regards what she does as asexual, 'pure' love, since, after all, she carefully avoids applying more excitations to the child's genitals than are unavoidable in nursery care. As we know, however, the sexual drive is not aroused only by direct excitation of the genital zone. What we call affection will unfailingly show its effects one day on the genital zones as well. Moreover, if the mother understood more of the high importance of the part played by instincts in mental life as a whole – in all its ethical and psychical achievements – she would spare herself any self-reproaches even after her enlightenment. She is only fulfilling her task in teaching the child to love. After all, he is meant to grow up into a strong and capable person with vigorous sexual needs and to accomplish during his life all the things that human beings are urged to do by their drives. It is true that an excess of parental affection does harm by causing precocious sexual maturity and also because, by spoiling the child, it makes him incapable in later life of temporarily doing without love or of being content with a smaller amount of it. One of the clearest indications that a child will later become neurotic is to be seen in an insatiable demand for his parents' affection. And on the other hand, neuropathic parents, who are inclined as a rule to display excessive affection, are precisely those who are most likely by their caresses to arouse the child's disposition to neurotic illness.

Extract 7: From *Three Essays on the Theory of Sexuality*, *SE* 7, pp. 222–3

With this passage we arrive at the infamous Freud of popular imagination, the Freud who propounds the scandalously unpalatable notion of incestuous attachment as a prototype for adult love, the Freud who contaminates the cherished innocence of childhood and parental affection with sexual desire. The outlandish, disreputable, perverse Freud.

Of course, love and sex have already peeped from behind the black veils of neurotic symptoms, slips, dreams and the uncanny. Displacements, condensations, negations, along with all the other mechanisms of the unconscious, defend against the direct revelation of inadmissible desires and excessive drives. Love, we've discovered, consigns us to perpetual, though unwitting, dissimulation.

Our passage is extracted from a section of the third of Freud's magisterial *Three Essays on the Theory of Sexuality* of 1905, entitled 'The Finding of an Object'. It's immediately preceded by the following sentences: 'There are . . . good reasons why a child sucking at his [we should note the gender-neutrality of the German word *kind* – unlike Strachey's translation, Freud's original doesn't specify the child as male] mother's breast has become the prototype of every relation of love. The finding of an object is in fact a *re*finding of it' (*SE* 7, p. 223).

How is this crucial but enigmatic distinction to be understood? First, it places the original object of love in the past rather than the future: sexual love doesn't arrive suddenly and unannounced at adolescence, but recovers and repeats (unconsciously) the (unconsciously) remembered love of and for the mother. Love is always in this sense a form of displacement, a disguised re-enactment of its first and irretrievable form. But does this then suggest that our earliest love-relation is the authentic original, to which all subsequent loves are inferior sequels? Is sexual love simply the doomed attempt to restore the idyllic unity of mother and child?

The present passage suggests otherwise. Freud, to be sure, stated unambiguously the profoundly formative force of the relation to the mother in the child's erotic development. But if his image of the baby at the breast conveys a sense of minds and bodies in perfect fusion, the subsequent passage hints at a rather more complicated and ambivalent set-up. For what's most striking about Freud's description of the loving mother is the sense that she's unaware of what she's *doing* when she loves: 'A mother would probably be horrified if she were made aware that all her marks of affection were rousing her child's sexual drive and preparing for its later intensity'. In other words, our first love is born of confusion – neither party fully understands the desire and motivation of the other. The baby inhabits a zone in which maternal and sexual love haven't yet been subjected to their strictly enforced separation. On the other hand, so deeply embedded is this separation in the mind of the mother that the suggestion she's breaching it would leave her 'horrified'. To the mother who's long since repressed it, the child's inner life is uncanny indeed.

This relationship of mutual misunderstanding, moreover, far from being left behind after childhood, helps shape all subsequent erotic relationships. Freud puts a positive gloss on this predicament in the passage under consideration. Enlighten the horrified mother of the formative role of her affection in 'teaching the child to love', he assures us, and 'she would spare herself any self-reproaches'. The assurance is rather fragile, however: whilst the stimulation of the child's erotic drives will nurture their capacities for both love and work – that is, make them worthy adults – an excess of it can result in 'precocious sexual maturity' and an insatiable and unrelenting sexual neediness.

Of course, there's no universal measure available by which to judge parental affection 'excessive' – such judgements are shaped by, and subject to the perpetual shifts of, culture and history. But the very problem of determining what constitutes this excess reveals just how central misunderstanding is to our erotic development. Mother and child are persistently vulnerable to confusing both the nature and the effect of the other's love (and, of course, of their love for the other). For children, the oppositions that organize adult reasoning haven't yet developed; they inhabit that zone of mental life where yes and no are 'unsplit', where the 'canny' hasn't undergone the alienation that gives rise to the uncanny. Here, love doesn't divide itself between different kinds of objects, and so doesn't take on distinct manifestations. The affectionate child, devoted parent, steadfast friend and passionate lover belong to later stages of mental life, by which the erotic drive has been subjected to the discipline of law and reason. Love, that is, learns to distinguish within itself different objectives and aims.

Loving as an adult, then, involves recognition of the prohibition separating parental from sexual love. But Freud's seminal contribution to the psychology of love was to show how this erotic discipline is built upon, and forever haunted by, the erotic *in*discipline of the child. Indeed, it's a necessary precondition for meaningful adult love that this haunting erotic undertow of childhood be paid its due, as Freud argued in his 1912 essay, 'On the Universal Tendency to Debasement in the Sphere of Love'. In what I think of as his single most startling sentence, he remarked of men: 'It sounds not only disagreeable but also paradoxical, yet it must nevertheless be said that anyone who is to be really free and happy in love must have surmounted his respect for women and have come to terms with the idea of incest with his mother or sister' (*SE* 11, p. 186).

We may be tempted to ask, not for the first time, why we

should accept such a distasteful thesis. What possible relationship could there be between happy love and the contemplation of incest? Any response to this question has to begin from one of Freud's most fundamental yet (by his own admission) elusive concepts: the drive. It's a term we've already invoked in previous chapters without worrying unduly about its meaning. But it's necessary to define the precise nature of the drive if we're to make sense of the Freudian model of sexuality.

The difficulty with such precise definition, he tells us at the outset of his great 1915 essay, 'Drives and Their Vicissitudes', is that the concept itself, whilst 'indispensable', is 'somewhat obscure' (*SE* 14, p. 118). We can begin to bring the hazy contours of this concept into focus by referring both to the original German word *Trieb* and its translation as 'instinct' throughout Strachey's *Standard Edition*. Anglophone psychoanalytic thinkers and translators now tend to insist, as we do here, on translating *Trieb* as 'drive'. The first argument in favour of this move is that *Trieb* must be precisely distinguished from instinct (whose German equivalent is in fact *Instinkt*). Instinct is a kind of self-preservative knowledge genetically encoded in non-human animals, which endows the animal with the abilities to feed, defend, shelter and reproduce itself with little or no prior parental care or training.

Human sexuality, the *Three Essays* suggest, is not an instinct in this respect, for neither its *aim* nor its *object* (two key terms introduced in the *Three Essays*) is exclusive. It is constituted rather by a drive, a constant pressure on the human organism exerted from within and clamouring for satisfaction. Where the path to instinctive satisfaction in the animal is fixed and direct, drives are rather more inclined to diversion. This tendency introduces a fascinating tension into

Freud's *Three Essays*, one which is implicit in the passage under discussion.

On the one hand, the book insists that human sexuality contains within itself an ultimate aim which defines, 'the normal sexual life of the adult, in which the pursuit of pleasure comes under the sway of the reproductive function' (*SE* 7, p. 197). From this perspective, whilst erotic pleasure may be stimulated by any number of bodily zones (the mouth, the anus, the eyes, the limbs) and their attendant activities (sucking, biting, excreting, looking, touching), Freud saw these 'component drives' as finally falling 'under the primacy of a single erotogenic zone [the genitals]' and 'directed towards a sexual aim attached to some extraneous sexual object' (*SE* 7, p. 197). This notion of genital primacy is a telling index of an abidingly functionalist, even mechanistic, tendency in Freud's understanding of the human organism. The infinitely various modes of erotic expression in human life are validated only inasmuch as they serve the biological end of reproduction. Kissing, looking and touching are simply way-stations on the journey to the procreative destination.

On the other hand, Freud couldn't help noting the sheer *fragility* of the genital organisation. Far from mapping out a one-way passage to 'some extraneous sexual object', that is, to a man or woman with whom we reproduce, the erotic drive is radically mobile, perpetually attaching (or in Freud's phrase, *soldering*) itself to and detaching itself from a potentially infinite range of objects across the course of our lives. It was his study of sexual perversions that alerted Freud to this essential feature of 'normal' sexual life. Perversions, he contends, are sexual behaviours that privilege the means over the end, by fixating either on bodily zones other than the genital or on erotic activities that, rather than being lingered over, 'should normally be traversed rapidly on the path towards final sexual union' (*SE* 7, p. 150).

And yet, as Freud himself implied, his very attempt to distinguish the perverse from the normal brings the two into inevitable proximity – by his definition, he can't help noting, even kissing falls under the category of the perverse. The opposition of normal to perverse remains stable only as long as we think of sexuality as an *instinct*, as a piece of knowledge biologically encoded in and reflexively discharged by the human organism. But Freud's innovation in the theory of sexuality was precisely to conceive the fundament of erotic life as an aimless and fickle *drive*, for which both the body and the external world provide infinitely various sources of pleasure. Insofar as sexuality is a drive, then, all sexuality, including its 'normal' form, is by its very nature perverse.

Despite appearances, we haven't strayed too far outside the boundaries of our passage. For what does this account of the mother–child relation reveal if not the formative force of the drive in our erotic development? If we thought of this relation in instinctive terms, we'd find in it a kind of ideal symmetry – an economically precise quantity, and mutually appropriate quality, of love passing between mother and child. Drives, however, are not so tidy. As most of us know, love, and especially the love that exists between parents and children, refuses to conform to any measure or limit (the very same, in fact, can be said of hate). The carer's ministrations afford the child 'an *unending* source of sexual excitation and satisfaction', whilst the child in turn awakens in the parent a similarly excessive desire. This is a qualitative as much as a quantitative excess: for both child and mother it spills over the boundaries between affection and lust, maternal and sexual. The child's 'affection and esteem' for his carer is indistinguishable from 'sexual love', whilst casual observation makes it 'quite clear' that the mother treats her baby 'as a substitute for a complete sexual object'.

The drive, said Freud, is a concept 'lying on the frontier between the mental and the physical' (*SE* 7, p. 168). It is this borderline status that makes the drive such a destabilizing force. On the one hand, without reinforcement by the visceral immediacy of the body's desires, a drive would be indistinguishable from a thought, albeit a compelling one; but equally, without reinforcement by the uncanny power of phantasy, the drive would be a mere transitory physical sensation. The love between parent and child is 'drive-love', a delirious crossing of physical craving and mental yearning, each as insatiable as the other.

Freud suggested in the passage that this love can be either nourishing or ruinous, but it may be more precise to argue that it's both nourishing *and* ruinous, both necessary and damaging to our erotic growth. Without it, we can never learn to love as adults, but as a result of it, adult love is prone to perpetual confusion and misunderstanding. For our passage teaches that the 'prototype of every relation of love', the breastfeeding mother and the suckling baby, destines love to be modelled on confusion, on excessive and uncontainable desires. Freud discovered this disturbing truth about love not in theoretical speculation, but in the knotty transactions of the consulting room, and gave it the name of *transference*.

As with so many of his discoveries, it was hysteria that first hinted at this phenomenon. As early as his publication *Studies on Hysteria*, Freud had observed that in clinical treatment, repressed impulses of love, hate and fear would repeat themselves in distorted form as 'impulses toward the analyst'. A hysterical patient, he reports, was in the grip of a repressed wish from years earlier that the man she was interested in would kiss her. Then, 'on one occasion ... a similar wish came up in her mind about me' (*SE* 2, p. 303). What this 'false connection' between the original love-object and the analyst showed was that our drives are apt to be transferred from one context to another. The relationship between analyst and patient only crystallized the mysterious compulsion of love to manifest itself as the unconsciously disguised repetition of its earlier forms. When we say of our friends (we're rarely courageous enough to notice it about ourselves) that, 'they always go for the same kind of people' or 'make the same mistakes in their relationships', we're taking note of just this phenomenon.

The analytic situation brings this hidden phenomenon into the painfully bright light of day. The patient's singular combinations of needy dependence, loving esteem, sexual passion, hateful resentment and rebellious rejection of the analyst all repeat the patterns that her particular history of loving and hating creates. Lurking behind these repetitions, of course, is the great 'prototype of every relation of love'. Thus it is that, 'the finding of an object is in fact a *re*finding of it'. But what our reading of this passage should have shown is that the 'prototype' of love doesn't relate to its later childhood, adolescent and adult transferences as a pristine original does to its pale copy, or as clarity does to confusion. For where love's concerned, the prototype is no less confused and confusing than its derivatives. Love is born in confusion, in misdirected aims against misperceived objects.

Freud made this point very strikingly in his 1915 essay 'Observations on Transference-Love', the last in *Papers on Technique*. Should the analyst tell the patient, he asked, that the love she (in Freud's accounts, transference-love is always that of a female patient for a male analyst) bears him is simply illusory, 'entirely composed of repetitions and copies of earlier reactions, including infantile ones' (*SE* 12, p. 167)? This, he responds, is to miss the point about love itself. The repetition of 'old traits' and 'infantile reactions' is 'the essential character of *every* [my emphasis] state of being in love'(*SE* 12, p. 168). In other words, what the transference-love of patient for analyst reveals is that all love is transference. Because we never 'found', or fully possessed, our object in the first place, the process of 'refinding' it, or indeed of transferring it, is never really fulfilled: 'It is my belief', proclaimed Freud in 'On the Universal Tendency to Debasement', 'that, however strange it may sound, we must reckon with the possibility that something in the nature of the sexual drive itself is unfavourable to the realization of complete satisfaction' (*SE* 11, pp. 188–9). Love is the reappearance, in disguise, of its previous disguises.

I'll conclude this discussion of the vicissitudes of love with a brief reading of a profound fictional meditation on the subject, which also happens to be a joke. It comes from *Two Jews on a Train*, Adam Biro's 1998 gathering and inspired rewriting of comic European Jewish stories[9]. 'Sex' begins (of course) with the meeting of two Parisian Jews, 'Friedländer and Bensimon', on a train. After an ostentatious display of mutual affection, they settle into more intimate conversation. The demonstrative Bensimon coaxes from his more reserved friend the reason for his troubled demeanour. Friedländer hints tentatively at marital problems, before being cajoled by his companion into blurting out that Sarah 'doesn't like *it* . . . *It, it,* you know, going to bed, sex, fucking!" (p. 82). There follows a frenzied confessional monologue, in which he complains about his beautiful wife's symptoms of sexual withdrawal: she shows no interest, walks around the house in a baggy old sweater and apron, goes to bed in an ugly nightgown.

The self-possessed Bensimon determines to resolve the problem. Overcoming his friend's hesitation, he undertakes to speak to Sarah himself, which he does as soon as Friedländer leaves the train. Sarah's response to Bensimon's reproaches is appropriately forthright: 'Daniel lives for his mother' (p. 84). Holidays, she elaborates, are spent with his mother at her country homes, she's with them for dinner every Friday night, her husband calls her every morning and evening, their daughter is named after her: 'She is between us, at our table, in Daniel's head, and obviously even in our bed. So I, I have given up.' (p. 85).

Not one to quit, Bensimon counters her exasperated response with a desperate and heartfelt appeal to her to 'reconquer Daniel', to seduce him with perfume, lace and liquour. The appeal, despite the embarrassment it causes her, succeeds. Sarah ventures out to buy herself, 'the sexiest, most provocative lingerie she can find' from Christian Dior, shrouds herself in a cloud of bewitching fragrance, and, in their seductively darkened living room, awaits her husband with trembling anticipation, in a casually lascivious pose. Friedländer enters, and the story ends with his reaction: 'What's going on? What's this small lamp – why don't you turn on the big one? Oh my God, what's happening? Why are you dressed in black? Did something happen to Mom?' (p. 86).

Of course, a psychoanalytic gloss on this story is strictly superfluous – it's already done that work itself. What more hilariously tragic affirmation could there be that, 'anyone who is to be really happy in love . . . must have come to terms with the idea of incest with his mother' (*SE* 11, p. 186)?

Friedländer's erotic growth has been stunted by an inability to do just this. Concealed in his sequence of terrified questions is the unresolved unconscious memory of a child's love for the mother who 'helps him in his helplessness'. Dependence, our passage tells us, engenders an erotic attachment which doesn't distinguish the affectionate from the sexual. A successfully 'dissolved' Oedipus complex, Freud will later tell us, involves the child's acceptance of the impossibility of fulfilling their desire for their mother. Initially (in the 'latency' period) this results in the child's total renunciation of desire. When this lost infantile desire returns in adolescence, it is diverted – or transferred – to new objects.

For reasons the story thankfully doesn't attempt to provide, this diversion of desire from mother to other has gone awry for Friedländer. He finds intolerable the unconscious knowledge that adult desire has its source in its infantile prototype. Freud had identified this common masculine predicament in his essay on debasement: 'where they love they do not desire and where they desire they cannot love' (*SE* 11, p. 183).

What Freud's essay on debasement and Biro's story reveal in their indispensably different ways is the self-defeating nature of the attempt to think that the difference between affectionate and sexual love as one of strict opposition. The man who can't desire and love simultaneously is one who can't bear the unconscious memory of a time when he didn't know the difference. He expresses a profound resistance to the obscurity of his desire, to the disconcertingly intimate relation of 'free and happy love' to 'the idea of incest'. The illusory opposition between love and desire, a doomed attempt to make the world clearer, can only make the world more perplexingly and miserably obscure, as Friedländer's climactic questions so vividly attest. To the man who 'lives for his mother', erotic darkness and seductive lingerie are doomed to be misrecognised as signs of mourning. Paradoxically, a free and happy love is achieved only when we accept the incestuous desire to which we're unconsciously bound.

8

THE OBSCURER OBJECT OF DESIRE

The first auto-erotic sexual satisfactions are experienced in connection with vital functions which serve the purpose of
self-preservation. The sexual drives are at the outset attached to
the satisfaction of the ego-drives; only later do they become inde-
pendent of these, and even then we have an indication of that
original attachment in the fact that the persons concerned with a
child's feeding, care, and protection become his earliest sexual
objects: that is to say, in the first instance his mother or a substitute for her. Side by side, however, with this type and source of
object-choice, which may be called the 'anaclitic' or 'attachment'
type, psycho-analytic research has revealed a second type, which
we were not prepared for finding. We have discovered, especially
clearly in people whose libidinal development has suffered some
disturbance, such as perverts and homosexuals, that in the later
choice of love-objects they have taken as a model not their
mother but their own selves. They are plainly seeking *themselves*
as a love-object, and are exhibiting a type of object-choice which
must be termed 'narcissistic'. In this observation we have the
strongest of the reasons which have led us to adopt the hypothesis of narcissism.

We have, however, not concluded that human beings are divided into two sharply differentiated groups, according as their object-choice conforms to the anaclitic or the narcissistic type; we assume rather that both kinds of object-choice are open to each individual, though he may show a preference for one or the other. We say that a human being has originally two sexual objects – himself and the woman who nurses him – and in doing so we are postulating a primary narcissism in everyone, which may in some cases manifest itself in a dominating fashion in his object-choice.

A comparison of the male and female sexes then shows that there are fundamental differences between them in respect of their type of object-choice, although these differences are of course not universal. Complete object-love of the attachment type is, properly speaking, characteristic of the male. It displays the marked sexual overvaluation which is doubtless derived from the child's original narcissism and thus corresponds to a transference of that narcissism to the sexual object. This sexual overvaluation is the origin of the peculiar state of being in love, a state suggestive of a neurotic compulsion, which is thus traceable to an impoverishment of the ego as regards libido in favour of the love-object. [. . .] Women, especially if they grow up with good looks, develop a certain self-contentment which compensates them for the social restrictions that are imposed upon them in their choice of object. Strictly speaking, it is only themselves that such women love with an intensity comparable to that of the man's love for them. Nor does their need lie in the direction of loving, but of being loved; and the man who fulfils this condition is the one who finds favour with them. Such women have the greatest fascination for men, not only for aesthetic reasons, since as a rule they are the most beautiful, but also because of a combination of interesting psychological factors. For it seems very

evident that another person's narcissism has a great attraction for
those who have renounced part of their own narcissism and are in
search of object-love. The charm of a child lies to a great extent
in his narcissism, his self-contentment and inaccessibility, just as
does the charm of certain animals which seem not to concern
themselves about us, such as cats and the large beasts of prey.
Indeed, even great criminals and humorists, as they are represented in literature, compel our interest by the narcissistic
consistency with which they manage to keep away from their ego
anything that would diminish it. It is as if we envied them for
maintaining a blissful state of mind – an unassailable libidinal
position which we ourselves have abandoned. The great charm of
narcissistic women has, however, its reverse side; a large part of
the lover's dissatisfaction, of his doubts of the woman's love, of
his complaints of her enigmatic nature, has its root in this incongruity between the types of object-choice.

Extract from 'On Narcissism', *SE* 14, pp. 87–9

As if it weren't shocking enough that an adult turns out to be
derived from infantile sexuality, we're informed by this passage
from the 1914 essay 'On Narcissism' that infantile sexuality is
itself derived from a prior source. Freud's characterisation of
the baby at the breast as prototype of every love-relation
implied that the erotic drive first reveals itself in the infant's
love for his carer. Our passage from 'On Narcissism', however,
complicates the picture, for where the passage from *Three
Essays* intimates that the mother is the infant's first and exclusive object of desire, the theory of narcissism suggests a rival is
in place before she comes on the scene – the infant himself.

Self-love, or 'auto-eroticism', Freud claimed in the first
paragraph, precedes the love of another. But what drives self-
love in its earliest form isn't self-regard but self-preservation. A

baby's first forms of auto-erotic indulgence, notably the sucking of his thumb and lips, express a kind of primitive and
involuntary submission to the imperative of his own care:
'The sexual drives are at the outset attached to the satisfaction
of the ego-drives'. Self-stimulation, from the mouth to the
genitals, is a means by which the baby becomes its own erotic
object, that is, an object worth looking after.

What Freud had earlier referred to as the love of infants for
'those who help them in their helplessness' is now revealed as
the extension and transformation of their auto-erotic attachment to themselves. The child's 'earliest sexual objects' are
chosen precisely because they answer to his demand of self-
preservation better than he can himself. For this reason,
self-love can't be rigidly opposed to the love of another: the
latter is always conditioned by the former. Quite simply, the
infant returns only the love he receives.

In the later erotic life of the individual, this self-love will be
periodically revived in the form of 'narcissism'. The narcissist
loves only insofar as his object reflects back to him, as in the
original Narcissus myth, his own image. Freud seems to suggest here that narcissistic is in some way more fundamental
than anaclitic (Strachey's rather technical translation of the
German *Anlehnung* – literally 'leaning on') love. Narcissistic
love is first of all, and in fact never ceases to be, self-love. The
infant's attachment to another only extends his attachment to
himself. This has a number of important implications for our
understanding of the erotic drive, which we'll duly address.
Before so doing, however, it's worth asking to what extent we
should accept Freud's key premise.

Certainly, the most casual experience and examination of
self and others can't fail to yield evidence of a strong narcissistic strain in every one of us. And yet I can't help feeling

sceptical towards the postulation of a self-preservative drive older and more essential than the erotic drive. For if attachment to another is an effect of attachment to the self, isn't the reverse equally true? Isn't the love of self also a reflection of the love of others? When Freud wrote that, 'the sexual drives are at the outset attached to the satisfaction of the ego-drives', he suggests a certain sequence in my relation to the world. According to this story, I discover my self and its demands first, and others 'only later'. Something about the neatness of this story doesn't quite ring true. It implies that the self is formed prior to and outside of its relations with others. But isn't it the case that I'm already *in* relationships as soon as, and indeed before, I come into the world? The baby's biological dependence on the mother inside the womb, and helplessness once it emerges from it, mean that its selfhood can never be dissociated from the presence of others. Insofar as we're able to talk about the newborn baby's 'experience', we can say that it's characterized by a blurring of the boundaries between itself and others. Does it make sense in this context to speak of ego-drives operating 'before' erotic drives? Isn't it precisely the baby's inability to identify where he ends and the other begins that renders his world so uncanny to us? Freud was undoubtedly right to claim that there's no attachment without narcissism. But there's equally no narcissism without attachment – self-love enforces and is enforced by the love of an object.

This is more than hair-splitting, for it has direct bearing on Freud's characterization of different forms of sexual behaviour, notably homosexuality. The narcissist, according to his model, cannot direct love outwards. All the love he receives becomes so much grist to the mill of self-love (as in that great conversational gambit, 'Enough about me, what about you? What do *you* think of me?'). According to our passage, this predicament lies at the basis of the libidinal development of 'perverts and homosexuals', among others 'whose libidinal development has suffered some disturbance'.

The intimate tie between homosexuality and narcissism was first posited in his 1910 biographical study of Leonardo Da Vinci (*Leonardo Da Vinci and a Memory of His Childhood*). Freud argued, on the basis of biographical speculation on Leonardo's early childhood, that homosexuality arises when the child is made to repress his attachment to his mother: 'The boy represses his love for his mother: he puts himself in her place, identifies himself with her, and takes his own person as a model in whose likeness he chooses the new objects of his love' (*SE* 11, p. 100). Prevented by his own repression from returning the love he receives, the boy instead redirects his desire for his mother inward. This is an act of *identification*, by which he aligns his self-perception with his mother's, and so becomes an object of his own love. The boys whom he comes to love, 'are after all only substitutive figures and revivals of himself in childhood – boys whom he loves the way his mother loved *him* [Freud's emphasis] when he was a child' (*SE* 11, p. 100). The homosexual, on this view, is really his mother in disguise.

If there's a false note in the sentence just cited, it's the word 'only'. To characterise the homosexual's objects as 'only' substitutive figures is to imply that certain objects are *more* than substitutive. Isn't such a premise quite untenable from a psychoanalytic perspective? In the previous chapter, we discovered via the concept of transference that the disguised repetition of infantile patterns of relating is 'the essential character of *every* state of being in love' (*SE* 12, p. 168). In other words, homosexual love is no less authentic for being disguised self-love (if indeed Freud is right to claim that's what it is) than is heterosexual love for being disguised incestuous love. To characterize homosexual love as a 'disturbance' on the basis that it's a disguise is to forget that all love is disguise – and no less real for that. On the contrary, we might say that Freud teaches us to view disguise as the very sign and seal of emotional reality.

Perhaps the problem here is a certain tension in Freud's thinking between different ways of knowing. On the one hand, we can detect the peculiar zeal of the nineteenth-century scientist for a taxonomical order which would bring the chaotic mass of particular cases under the discipline of the general rule. Thus arises the designation of certain types – homosexuals, good-looking women, humorists, cats – to narcissistic object-choices, and others (heterosexual men in particular) to the anaclitic.

On the other hand, Freud seemed to want to resist this temptation to generalize. Notice his unwillingness to divide the human race into rigidly opposed categories: 'We have, however, not concluded that human beings are divided into two sharply differentiated groups, according as their object-choice conforms to the anaclitic or the narcissistic type'. Moreover, the differences of the sexes with regard to 'their type of object-choice', whilst undoubtedly 'fundamental', are not 'universal'. In these hesitations and qualifications, Freud seemed to be edging away from generalized alignments of each type of object-choice with particular groups of people, and towards a deep understanding of the shallow truism that 'everyone's different'.

What the truism means in this case is that both narcissistic and anaclitic impulses are present in varying ratios in every individual, and that gender or sexual orientation can provide only the vaguest of hints as to what this ratio will be in any given individual. We can illustrate this argument by returning to Freud's example in the Leonardo study of the man who chooses to love substitute versions of himself as a result of the internalization of his mother's perspective. Surely there's no particular reason why such a substitute self should be of the same sex? On the contrary, don't we frequently see ourselves reflected in the faces of others – others strictly differentiated from us by gender, ethnicity, class, age, weight, dress-sense – for the most obscurely enigmatic reasons? Similarly, there's no particular reason why an intense love of the anaclitic type shouldn't be directed towards another of the same sex, or from a woman towards a man – the permutations are endless. Types of object-choice aren't predetermined by overarching categories of gender, sexuality or beauty, but are the outcome of the singularly rich internal and external histories of partic-ular individuals. There is simply no telling in advance who, how or why a person is going to love who they love.

None of this is intended as a denial of the phenomenon of narcissism itself; the point is rather that, as Freud himself remarked, there is no 'pure' form of either narcissistic or ana-clitic love: the one is always somehow bound up with the other. Indeed, Freud wrote towards the end of the essay that, 'a real happy love corresponds to the primal condition in which object-libido and ego-libido cannot be distinguished' (*SE* 14, p. 100). In such a love, there's no means of telling whether the love of another is disguising self-love or vice versa, and indeed, no reason why, if such a love is really happy, anyone should care. In our present passage, Freud wrote of a 'complete object-love of the attachment type . . . characteris-tic of the male', thinking of the romantic lover who prostrates himself before his adored and impossibly idealized (in Freud's wryly sceptical term 'overvalued') lady. But for all its outward appearance of self-sacrifice, could such a love not be interpreted as being at least as much narcissistic as anaclitic? After all, doesn't the state of being 'madly' in love consist above all in the lover's mistaking the reality of his beloved for his own self-serving phanatasies of who she is? Whether love is being directed towards self or other is never obvious, even (or especially) when it appears to be.

Still, there's no doubting the existence of narcissistic types. Freud falls back, for his exemplar, on the tired stereotype of the beautiful woman. But he adds some quirkier types to the list – children, big cats, 'criminals and humorists'. And he offers perhaps his earliest version of love as self-perpetuating sadomasochistic pact: the narcissist's consuming self-love meshes ideally with the anaclitic type's need to love another. But the match turns out to be far from harmonious; the very self-enclosure and indifference that drew the lover to his narcissistic object can only become a source of misery, yielding 'doubts of the woman's love' and 'complaints of her enigmatic nature'. The trials of loving a narcissist are bound to revive the lover's own sleeping, and now wounded and resentful, narcissism.

In *Totem and Taboo* (1913), his famous attempt to unearth the anthropological basis of the Oedipus complex, Freud described the narcissistic stage as the moment, 'at which the hitherto dissociated sexual drives come together into a single unity and cathect the ego as an object' (*SE* 13, p. 89). The baby's auto-erotic drives are initially diffuse, uncontained by any clear distinction between self and other, inside and outside. Narcissism draws these drives into a single 'unity', transforming the nebulous pleasure of auto-eroticism into the love of a defined object – the baby's own self. We are here in the heart of what Freud's most controversial psychoanalytic successor, Jacques Lacan, called the 'mirror stage', the moment at which, recognising his own image in a mirror (like Narcissus), the infant assumes 'the illusion of autonomy',[10] imposing an imaginary unity and self-sufficiency upon his own irremediable internal divisions and fractures. Before Lacan, Freud had argued that this 'narcissistic organisation is never wholly abandoned' (*SE* 13, p. 89). For some, indeed, it seems to persist with a peculiarly intense force. The beauty, criminal and humorist are all caught within that 'illusion of autonomy' which feeds their sense of omnipotent self-enclosure.

According to Donald Winnicott (perhaps the most important figure in British analysis after Freud), psychical health involves above all the delicate management of the infant's transition from this 'primary' narcissistic omnipotence to an acceptance of his separate and finite existence. Narcissism is a resistance to this transition, a refuge in the infantile illusion of his absolute power and independence.

Freud's seminal essay 'Mourning and Melancholia' (1917), argues that the fear of surrendering this illusory omnipotence lies at the base of melancholy, or what today we would call depression. Why, he asks, are certain individuals unable to 'work through' the loss of a loved object? What prevents them from completing the process of mourning and moving on? Freud had recourse in his response to the concept of identification discussed above. The melancholic is locked into his own unresolved grief because he experiences 'object-loss' as 'ego-loss' (*SE* 14, p. 249). Having loved his object on the basis of a narcissistic identification with her (or him), her absence is felt as an irremediable absence in himself, a loss that refuses to be compensated. The melancholic is a disillusioned narcissist, forced by the death or rejection of his loved object to come to terms with loss and separation as a necessary fact of life itself. His object of desire – his self in all its illusory unity and plenitude – is even more irretrievably obscure than the lost mother. An unspeakably bitter lesson: little wonder that some would turn to a career of vanity, crime or humour just to avoid accepting it.

9

THE OBSCUREST OBJECT OF DESIRE

Let us suppose, then, that all the organic drives are conservative, are acquired historically and tend towards the restoration of an earlier state of things. It follows that the phenomena of organic development must be attributed to external disturbing and diverting influences. The elementary living entity would from its very beginning have had no wish to change; if conditions remained the same, it would do no more than constantly repeat the same course of life. In the last resort, what has left its mark on the development of organisms must be the history of the earth we live in and of its relation to the sun. Every modification which is thus imposed upon the course of the organism's life is accepted by the conservative organic drives and stored up for further repetition. Those drives are therefore bound to give a deceptive appearance of being forces tending towards change and progress, whilst in fact they are merely seeking to reach an ancient goal by paths alike old and new. Moreover, it is possible to specify this final goal of all organic striving. It would be in contradiction to the conservative nature of the drives if the goal of life were a state of things which had never yet been attained. On the contrary, it must be an *old* state of things, an initial state from which the living entity has at one time or other departed and to which it is striving to return by the circuitous paths along which its development leads. If we are to take it as a truth that knows no exception that everything living dies for *internal* reasons – becomes inorganic once again – then we shall be compelled to say that '*the aim of all life is death*' and, looking backwards, that '*inanimate things existed before living ones*'.

The attributes of life were at some time evoked in inanimate matter by the action of a force of whose nature we can form no conception. It may perhaps have been a process similar in type to that which later caused the development of a consciousness in a particular stratum of living matter. The tension which then arose in what had hitherto been an inanimate substance endeavored to cancel itself out. In this way the first drive came into being: the instinct to return to the inanimate state. It was still an easy matter at that time for a living substance to die; the course of its life was probably only a brief one, whose direction was determined by the chemical structure of the young life. For a long time, perhaps, living substance was thus being constantly created afresh and easily dying, till decisive external influences altered in such a way as to oblige the still surviving substance to diverge ever more widely from its original course of life and make ever more complicated *détours* before reaching its aim of death. These circuitous paths to death, faithfully kept to by the conservative instincts, would thus present us to-day with the picture of the phenomena of life. If we firmly maintain the exclusively conservative nature of the drives, we cannot arrive at any other notions as to the origin and aim of life.

Extract from *Beyond the Pleasure Principle, SE* 18, pp. 37–9

The capacity to love both self and others attests, according to 'On Narcissism', to the human organism's 'two-fold existence'. I exist simultaneously as an individual concerned with my own preservation and pleasure, and as a member of the species concerned with its propagation and survival. But the text from which the current passage is extracted advances what may be Freud's audacious thesis: that the fundamental terms which make up this dual existence are not 'individual' and 'species' but 'life' and 'death'. *Beyond the Pleasure Principle* ventures the claim that an imperceptible drive to die lies behind our evident drive to live. Not the least extraordinary fact about this extraordinary book is its introduction of this momentous and transformative theoretical innovation so late in the sixty-five-year-old Freud's life and career.

The thesis of the *death-drive* remains the most controversial and contested of his concepts, reshaping our sense of Freud's own enterprise and opening up new and unexpected roads into the psychoanalytic future. For many in the mainstream of the analytic movement, the death-drive would remain outside the canon of Freud's key terms, an aberrant speculative digression, lacking the necessary grounding in empirical observation and research. For his bolder and more controversial successors, however (and I have in mind here thinkers as different as Melanie Klein and Jacques Lacan), it was the very excess, the conceptual 'madness' of the death-drive that made it such an inexhaustible resource for psychoanalytic thinking.

The love of others enables the species to reproduce itself, encourages the formation of communities and impels aesthetic and scientific achievement. This is the impulse, which Freud would name 'Eros', serving the interests of life (an impulse which encompasses, but can't be reduced to, what he earlier called the sexual drive). But attending to these interests demands serious physical, emotional and intellectual effort, a willingness to expose ourselves to myriad stimuli, pleasurable and painful, with which both the external world and our internal experience assail us.

The first chapter of Freud's 1920 text rehearses once more that principle of psychical economy first propounded in the 1895 'Project' and repeated at many points in the interim: 'the mental apparatus endeavours to keep the quantity of excitation in it as low as possible or at least to keep it constant' (*SE* 18, p. 9). Previously, however, Freud had associated this endeavour with the pleasure principle, whereby (let us recall) pleasure is proportionate to the extent to which stimulus has been minimized. *Beyond the Pleasure Principle* doesn't renounce this principle so much as endow it with a new and uncanny meaning.

We can make sense of this shift in meaning with the help of that universally familiar phenomenon of waking inertia. However energetic we imagine ourselves to be, however much we embrace the wealth of experiences daily life throws at us, the trials of getting up in the morning tell a different story. Something in us simply can't be bothered to face the day, would prefer to surrender to the lassitude of our heavy bodies and slow tongues. Our heads burrow into the pillow in protest against the disturbance induced by morning's noise and light.

Just what in us is speaking through this lassitude? Is this yet another manifestation of that uncanny 'someone else' emanating from the unconscious? If so, what is he, she, it, trying to say? Freud's disturbing answer is that it is expressing a drive to die. The wish to minimize tension derives from a wish to extinguish it, to return to the stasis of inorganic matter from whence we came and to which we'll return: 'all organic drives are conservative, are acquired historically and tend towards the restoration of an earlier state of things'.

This 'earlier state of things', according to Freud's speculative biology, is the inanimate condition which preceded the emergence of life and which is restored in death. The first part of our passage makes the fantastically counter-intuitive claim that, far from being opposed to the death-drive, the history of human life in all its radical changes and adaptations, is its secret expression.

'*Inanimate things existed before living ones*', wrote Freud. When inanimate matter is exposed to 'external disturbing and diverting influences', notably the sun, it is nudged into some rudimentary form of life. Now both visible evidence and common-sense intuition would seem to suggest that this life was driven from the beginning to its own growth, transformation and augmentation. And yet, Freud insisted, 'the elementary living entity would from its very beginning have no wish to change'. Living matter has, indeed, been forced by 'disturbing and diverting influence' into the profound evolutionary changes discovered by Darwin. But this is evidence less of an irrepressible life-force than of a 'conservative' drive to master and minimize change. The appearance life assumes of being impelled by the imperative of 'change and progress' is another, perhaps the most fundamental and devious, of the organism's many disguises, underneath which is concealed a compulsion to 'reach an ancient goal by paths alike old and new'. Or more simply: '*the aim of all life is death*'. From this estranged perspective, the pleasure-driven human of our advanced stage of evolution is simply the most recent disguise for the organism's impulse to 'die only in its own fashion' (*SE* 18, p. 39).

One irresistibly obvious objection we may wish to put to Freud is that the existence of a death-drive would ultimately manifest itself in the urge to kill ourselves at the first available opportunity. But this is to miss the importance for the organism of dying *only in its own fashion*. A death imposed from without will involve the very traumatic disturbance the organism is always seeking to avoid. It seems, rather pathetically perhaps, that it's less the fear of death that lies behind our aversion to suicide than fear of the knife, revolver or rope.

Once this suspicion of the death-driven substratum of life insinuated itself into Freud's thinking, he found it lurking in the most unexpected corners. In the book on jokes, for example, children's play was characterized, in line with society's most cherished mythologies, as innocent anarchy, an affirmative 'pleasure in nonsense' (*SE* 8, p. 125). Fifteen years later, in *Beyond's* most famous passage (one of the most famous in all of Freud, in fact), play comes under suspicion of rather more sinister motives. In this passage, Freud observes a toddler (his grandchild) throwing a bobbin over the edge of his cot 'so that it disappeared into it' (*SE* 18, p. 15). He accompanies this action with a 'loud, long-drawn-out "o-o-o-o"' (*SE* 18, p. 14), which Freud identified as representing the German '*fort*' ('gone'). The toddler then reels the bobbin out of the cot, greeting its reappearance 'with a joyful "*da*" ["there"]' (*SE* 18, p. 15).

Freud interpreted this game of 'disappearance and return' as the child's attempt to master, by means of repetitive re-enactment, the trauma of separation from his mother. Experience is forcing the realization that his mother is not an extension of himself, and can't be controlled in the manner of, say, his limbs. Apparently indifferent to his desire for her exclusive attention, she repeatedly leaves his presence for people and places unrelated to him, condemning him to a kind of incessant illusion of cuckoldry. The '*fort-da*' game is his playful representation of this everyday catastrophe.

But in what sense, Freud asked, could the repeated staging of this catastrophe 'fit in with the pleasure principle' (*SE* 18, p. 15)? Is a trauma not better forgotten than repeated? The problem with a forgotten trauma, of course, is that it's never quite forgotten. It leaves its trace in the unconscious, where it remains stubbornly inaccessible to its victim's memory and imagination. The victim of a forgotten (or repressed) trauma is thus condemned to *remain* a victim in his unconscious memory. Repetition, in contrast, harbours the magical power to transform what it repeats. The original separation was rendered the more traumatic for revealing to him his helpless *passivity* before it. The bobbin is a means of compensation for that passivity: 'by repeating it, unpleasurable though it was, as a game, he took on an *active* part' (*SE* 18, p. 16). The child's flailing arms, outstretched impotently towards his mother's retreating back, are transformed by the play–phantasy into the triumphant mastery of the bobbin.

Freud thus discovered in this most unlikely of settings the fundamental activity of the death-drive: the *compulsion to repeat*. Repetition is the (inadequate) means by which we seek to master the forces which exceed our power. By shifting from object to subject of the traumatic experience, we diminish, and distance ourselves from, its power to damage us.

First activated in play, the compulsion to repeat can continue to exert unconscious power over all the spheres and phases of our lives. In Chapter Seven, we discovered that the erotic drive was perpetually subject to the uncanny logic of transference: one love is always the disguised repetition of another. The compulsion to repeat suggests that the death-drive is no less liable to these diversions. And as with love, it is the relationship between analyst and patient that brings this liability to light. The patient transfers to the analyst, alongside the prototypes and earlier disguises of love, the deepest sources of psychic pain in the forms of aggression, shame, masochism, jealousy and megalomania. The patient may at one moment mock and scorn the analyst's power, at another cower abjectly under its threat, and at another attempt to sabotage the treatment itself. And of course, such transferences aren't confined to the four walls of the consulting room. Think of how readily our patterns of behaviour repeat themselves in spite of the lessons of experience: falling in love with the person most likely to abuse and undermine us, opening ourselves up to the friend who'll betray us, entering into new projects with happy abandon and ending them in frustrated failure – any one of us can make depressingly rich contributions to the list. A malignant gremlin appears to be at work in these recurrent disappointments, blocking our drive to embrace and expand life.

The compulsion to repeat, then, begins life as a drive to master the experiences and feelings that threaten our integrity and potency. But this drive, in defending against pain, sets itself equally against *learning*. The erotic drive exposes itself to the vicissitudes of life in the knowledge that their harsh lessons alone enable psychic change and growth. The death-drive's conservatism, in contrast, its desire to minimize the excitations endemic to the state of being alive, reminds us that the 'elementary living entity', which even now persists in us, 'had no wish to change'.

Our passage seems to suggest that even the most dramatic and unsettling gestures of change and development in a person's life are mere disguises for a deeper will to changelessness. As with the claim that love of another is always disguised narcissism, there's something infuriatingly self-confirming about this argument. Whether falling in love or out of it, taking or avoiding risks, living an active or sedentary life, it says, I'm always seeking to gain mastery over my experience, seeking one way or the other to minimize pain and disruption. This will to mastery is death-driven, inasmuch as it aspires to the 'final goal of organic striving', a state of eternal rest.

Can it really be that the large and small joys of living, the meals, paintings, conversations, kisses are all mere 'détours', little twists and turns on our 'circuitous paths to death'? Fortunately, Freud is alive to the absurdity of his argument's ultimate logic: 'But let us pause for a moment and reflect. It cannot be so' (*SE* 18, p. 39). Indeed it cannot, for this would be to relegate the erotic drive, the keystone of psychoanalytic thinking, to a secondary derivative of the death-drive. Pushing his extravagant biological speculations a little further, Freud instead imagined how the erotic would have gained independence of the death-drive. Among the 'elementary entities' of life were some, the 'germ-cells', that far from seeking the path of self-annihilation, pursued their own growth and development: 'These germ-cells, therefore, work against the death of the living substance and succeed in winning for it what we can only regard as potential immortality, though that may mean no more than a lengthening of the road to death' (*SE* 18, p. 40).

Notice the oscillation of tone within this one-sentence portrayal of the life-drive: in one clause the germ-cells of life promise 'potential immortality', in the next they merely prolong 'the road to death'. This abrupt shift between hubris and humility, between the potency and powerlessness of human life, perhaps best characterizes Freud's understanding of the two essential drives, and of the relationship between them. The paradox of this relationship can be illuminated by picking up on the telling observation in *Beyond* that only life drives are visible. When we look at human beings, we see them trying, with varying degrees of success, to live. When we come across the exception of the suicidal depressive, we say that she's lost the will to live, not that she's found the will to die. The death-drive can make itself visible (or otherwise accessible) to neither the casual observer nor the empirical researcher. Its silence and invisibility is what renders it simultaneously everything and nothing, a blank absence and an uncanny presence.

This inaccessibility is what pulled Freud back from the extreme claim that life works in the service of the death-drive. 'It cannot be so', because to make it so would be to endow the death-drive with the very determinacy and clarity it lacks. The death-drive is ominous not because we can see it, but because we *can't*. It doesn't show itself in the plain light of day, but insinuates itself imperceptibly into the texture of life, such that it's easily mistaken for its opposite. No wonder it took Freud so long to discover, or that he could adduce no direct empirical evidence for it – for the death-drive is what escapes when we try to look for it. It's one of the many great ironies of Freud's writings that the concept couched most explicitly in the language of biology is also the one that most resists scientific verification. Death's inaccessibility to experience renders it radically obscure – the obscurest of all objects of desire –indeed, one we're not even conscious of desiring.

But in what sense is a force so obscure 'there' at all? I'll conclude this chapter and venture an answer to this difficult question by way of some remarks on an advertising campaign – always an aggressively visible presence in contemporary culture, and in this case also *about* visibility. A French cosmetics corporation has recently been running a striking and very simple poster and television campaign for an anti-ageing cream. It consists of close-up black and white shots of the faces of beautiful women, overlaid by the mock hand-written slogan (or, on television, the voiced words), 'I'm 43', 'I'm 52' and so forth. Beneath we read the promise to 'give back ten years to the look of your skin'.

Admittedly, in an age of widespread genocidal terror, this seems a trivial, not to say mistaken, candidate for evidence of a death-drive in our culture. But the point here is to bring out not the most violent, but the most imperceptible and insidious manifestations of the drive. Anti-ageing creams would appear to be unambiguously on the side of life: they offer the promise of prolonging youthful beauty, and more distantly perhaps of extending longevity itself. What on earth should they have to do with death?

A first glance at the image yields uncomplicated surprise: she looks 33, and yet she's 43. Linger a little on the face, though, and a minutely yet decidedly different, a more convoluted impression emerges: *she looks like someone of 43 who looks 33*. That is, she looks, as the advert promises, like someone from whom ten years have been erased. What it seems not to have accounted for here is the uncanny effect of this erasure. Those years have disappeared, and yet one can't help feeling they're there, haunting the flawlessly smooth skin in their absence. The story the face tells doesn't quite ring true. It's the same story hinted at in a television ad for a rival company's similar product, in which the similarly youthful middle-aged model places a 'Do Not Disturb' sign on her door before retiring to bed. The 43-year-old face looks weirdly and inappropriately *undisturbed*, a flawless vessel emptied of its proper contents – life itself.

What the advert, one small manifestation of the massive

and omnipresent cult of extended youth, trades upon is the collective phantasy of erasing the fact of having *lived*, of being unburdened by 'external disturbing and diverting influences'. Here, under the innocuous cover of younger-looking skin, is the death-drive at work, silently intimating its ideal of a changeless, *lifeless* life.

The world we think we know is permanently estranged by reading Freud. It harbours everywhere a 'someone' or 'something' else beyond what's there to be seen and heard. This something else leaves us perpetually uncertain as to what we're seeing: me or my double? Love or self-love? Life or death? And what are we to make of the person for whom life-drive and death-drive, pleasure and pain, have become indistinguishable?

10

MASOCHISTIC ENDING

In my *Three Essays on the Theory of Sexuality*, in the section on the sources of infantile sexuality, I put forward the proposition that 'in the case of a great number of internal processes sexual excitation arises as a concomitant effect, as soon as the intensity of those processes passes beyond certain quantitative limits'. Indeed, 'it may well be that nothing of considerable importance can occur in the organism without contributing to the excitation of the sexual drive'. In accordance with this, the excitation of pain and unpleasure would be bound to have the same result too. The occurrence of such a libidinal sympathetic excitation when there is tension due to pain and unpleasure would be an infantile physiological mechanism which ceases to operate later on. It would attain a varying degree of development in different sexual constitutions; but in any case it would provide the physiological foundation on which the psychical structure of erotogenic masochism would afterwards be erected.

The inadequacy of this explanation is seen, however, in the fact that it throws no light on the regular and close connections of masochism and its counterpart in drive-life, sadism. If we go back a little further, to our hypothesis of the two classes of drives

which we regard as operative in the living organism, we arrive at
another derivation of masochism, which, however, is not in contradiction with the former one. In (multicellular) organisms the
libido meets the drive of death, or destruction, which is dominant
in them and which seeks to disintegrate the cellular organism and
to conduct each separate unicellular organism [composing it]
into a state of inorganic stability (relative though this may be).
The libido has the task of making the destroying drive innocuous,
and it fulfils the task by diverting that drive to a great extent outwards – soon with the help of a special organic system, the
muscular apparatus – the destructive drive, the drive for mastery,
or the will to power. A portion of this drive is placed directly in the
service of the sexual function, where it has an important part to
play. This is sadism proper. Another portion does not share in this
transposition outwards; it remains inside the organism and, with
the help of the accompanying sexual excitation described above,
becomes libidinally bound there. It is in this portion that we have
to recognize the original, erotogenic masochism.

We are without any physiological understanding of the ways
and means by which this taming of the death-drive by the libido
may be effected. So far as the psycho-analytic field of ideas is
concerned, we can only assume that a very extensive fusion and
amalgamation, in varying proportions, of the two classes of drives
takes place, so that we never have to deal with pure life drives or
pure death drives but only with mixtures of them in different
amounts. Corresponding to a fusion of drives of this kind, there
may, as a result of certain influences, be a *de*fusion of them. How
large the portions of the death drives are which refuse to be
tamed in this way by being bound to admixtures of libido we
cannot at present guess.

If one is prepared to overlook a little inexactitude, it may be
said that the death drive which is operative in the organism –

primal sadism – is identical with masochism. After the main portion of it has been transposed outwards on to objects, there
remains inside, as a residuum of it, the erotogenic mascochism
proper, which on the one hand has become a component of the
libido and, on the other, still has the self as its object. This
masochism would thus be evidence of, and a remainder from, the
phase of development in which the coalescence, which is so
important for life, between the death drive and Eros took place.

Extract from 'The Economic Problem of Masochism', *SE* 19,
pp. 163–4

Before 1920, Freud had conceived the human organism as
governed by the pleasure principle, the imperative to max-
imise pleasure and minimize its opposite. The theory of the
death-drive, however, both disturbs this principle and draws
us beyond it, into a zone of experience where the tidy opposition between pleasure and unpleasure hasn't yet taken hold.
We can hardly characterize the toddler's *fort-da* game as pleasurable, for by means of it he relived the trauma of separation.
And yet 'painful' is an equally inadequate description, for the
game was his means of mastering (and so reducing the force
of) that same trauma. The game confounds the distinction
between the two terms, hinting at some primordial phase of
the organism in which they were, to recall Celan, 'unsplit'.

It's this 'unsplit' relation between pleasure and pain that
Freud's 'economic' model of mental functioning can't
acknowledge. If pleasure consists in the avoidance or mini-
mization of unpleasure, it follows that the two are definitively
'split', rigidly separate from one another. As an expression of
the pleasure principle, sexuality would then consist in *keeping*
them separate.

But as we learn from our present and final passage, sexuality isn't always so principled: *masochistic* sexuality, on the contrary, is defined by its disturbance of the pleasure principle, its obliviousness to the basic distinction on which it rests. 'The Economic Problem of Masochism' is Freud's attempt to address this disturbance – a disturbance not only of the pleasure principle but of the theoretical coherence of psychoanalysis itself. The very title of his essay registers this threat: for the economic model of the mind, masochism is a *problem* – 'mysterious from the economic point of view'. The 'problem', as his understated opening acknowledges, is this: if pain is *opposed* to pleasure, how can it ever be a *source* of pleasure? Masochism seems to defy economic rationality. The pleasure principle had assured us we were thrifty house-keepers at heart ('economy', from the Greek *oikonomos* – literally, 'law of the home'), aiming at a tidily balanced psychical budget: just as we take on only the expenditure we can afford in our financial lives, so we take on only the stimulus we can discharge in our sexual lives. In contrast (rather like the ideal citizen of today's credit-based economy), the masochist always consumes more than he can afford, taking pleasure in the very act of exceeding his means – that is, in pain.

From the point of view of the pleasure principle, 'desiring pain' is mere logical nonsense, a contradiction in terms. But in the words of his teacher Charcot, repeatedly quoted by Freud: La théorie c'est bon; mais ça n'empêche pas d'exister (*SE* 3, p. 13). No amount of theoretical assurance that we don't desire our own pain, however persuasive, can prevent masochism from existing. Ever mindful of Charcot's lesson, Freud squarely confronts this inconvenient fact squarely.

Early on in the essay, Freud distinguishes three kinds of masochism: *erotogenic*, *feminine* and *moral*. He immediately goes on to argue that, 'the first . . . lies at the basis of the other two'

(*SE* 19, p. 161). In other words that 'feminine' passivity and excessive moral piety are both derivatives of an erotic 'pleasure in pain'. His concern in our passage is with this primary, erotic dimension of masochism.

In the paragraphs immediately preceding the extract, Freud enumerates some of the commonest masochistic practices and phantasies: 'being gagged, bound, painfully beaten, whipped, in some way maltreated, forced into unconditional obedience, dirtied and debased'. The common denominator of such desires is 'obvious . . . the masochist wants to be treated like a small and helpless child' (*SE* 19, p. 162). Obvious or not, the observation is striking, pointing to our original condition of helplessness as a source of compulsive sexual pleasure. Moreover, there is an intimate affinity between this infantile helplessness and the 'female situation' of 'being castrated, being copulated with, or giving birth to a baby' (*SE* 19, p. 162). For the masochist, these radically passive experiences are the ultimate lure. But didn't the *fort-da* game reveal our primordial fear of helplessness, alongside our equally primordial need to master it? Why then would helplessness be revived in the adult as an object of intense erotic desire?

The passage begins with Freud's recollection of a proposition regarding infantile sexuality in the *Three Essays* that, 'nothing of considerable importance can occur in the organism without contributing to the excitation of the sexual drive'. For the infant, on this view, all internal stimuli, whatever else they may be (painful, curious, funny), are also sexual: the relevant section of the *Three Essays* invokes 'swinging', 'being thrown up in the air' and 'railway-travel' (*SE* 7, pp. 201–202) as sources of infantile 'co-excitation'. This potentially infinite diversity of sources for sexual excitement is gradually diminished in the course of the child's development. The 'polymorphously perverse' infant's capacity to be excited almost anywhere, and by almost anything, falls victim to the external world's confinement of sexuality to appropriate times, places and body-parts.

Freud's economic model of sexuality is arguably a *symptom* of this process of repression. After all, it's premised on a distinction between pleasure and pain which is far less clear-cut in the mind of the infant. A nice irony: the repression of infantile sexuality which conditions the adult also, and no doubt unconsciously, shaped Freud's understanding of sexual pleasure. Doesn't his mechanistic understanding of sex as a means of discharging excitation and restoring the equilibrium of tension in the body betray a forgetting of the chaotic indiscipline of infantile sexuality? Put another way: isn't there something peculiarly *sexless* about sexuality as defined by the pleasure principle?

Genital sexuality, according to Freud the culmination of our erotic development, is libidinal energy in its most tightly *bound* form, binding being his term for the directing of energy into a restricted, cohesive organisation. Masochism, in contrast, is a radically unbound form of sexuality. It returns the adult to the intense passivity and bodily receptivity of the infant, to a time before the separation of pain from pleasure so central to the regulation of the libido.

The theory of co-excitation, then, was Freud's first attempt to make sense of this bleeding of pain into pleasure. Twenty years later, however, he found something lacking in it: 'it throws no light', as the passage says, on 'the regular and close connections of masochism and its counter part in drive-life, sadism'. This is in fact another way of saying that the death-drive, the major theoretical innovation of the intervening years, is missing from the earlier theory. The passage goes on to account for sadism and masochism as different, and intricately related, consequences of the encounter between the life- and death-drives.

In fact, the theory of masochism had undergone a number of intermediate steps before the position arrived at in 1925. In his account of the 'Wolf-Man' case, published in 1918, Freud unearthed from his analysis of a young and wealthy Russian man an intricate complex of childhood neuroses. Especially concerned with the vicissitudes of his erotic development, he used the case to show the dizzying regressions, inversions and oscillations to which the infantile sexual drive is constantly subject. Masochism was one among this convoluted story's many chapters. Freud reconstructed the process by which the explicit threat of castration, levelled against his patient as a child approaching the genital phase, had led to a frightened regression to the phase of 'anal' eroticism. The anal phase, derived from the child's pleasure in the power conferred on him by the retention and expulsion of his faeces, expressed itself in the child in the form of intense irritability and cruelty to animals. This sadism in turn gave way to phantasies of 'boys being chastised and beaten, and especially beaten on the penis' (*SE* 17, p. 26). In Freud's interpretation, the true subject of the beating phantasy was the boy himself: as is the way of drives, aggression is reversed, 'turned round . . . against himself . . . and converted into masochism' (*SE* 17, p. 26).

The suggestion here, elaborated in greater detail in Freud's essay of the following year on beating phantasies ('A Child Is Being Beaten'), is that masochism is a secondary phenomenon, a derivative of sadism. On this account, there is no 'primary masochism': phantasies of passively received pain and humiliation are substitutive disguises for a more primary aggression.

All this changes once masochism is thought in relation to the death-drive. Returning to our passage, we discover the death-drive pursuing its original aim of 'disintegrating' the organism. Sadism is the result of the libido's attempt at thwarting this aim, at 'making the destroying drive innocuous' by diverting it outwards. My libido is in this sense ruthlessly self-preservative: it knows someone has to be the victim of the death-drive, and would rather you than me. Thus, the discovery of a 'beyond' of the pleasure principle reverses the conception of masochism as disguised sadism. Now, on the contrary, 'primal sadism – is identical with masochism'.

Sadism is thus the triumph of libido over the death-drive, masochism of the death-drive over libido. Triumph not in the sense that either fully eliminates the other, but in the sense that one is made to take on the *form* of the other. In masochism, sexuality is taken over by an impulse to self-destruction which, as both psychoanalytic and pornographic literature have plentifully attested, can reach well beyond the 'playful' dimensions to which Freud confines it in this essay. Thus, whilst 'we never have to deal with pure life drives or pure death drives but only with mixtures of them in different amounts', masochism's particular formula for this mixture is heady with the intoxicating force of the latter.

Masochism reveals the infinitely strange ways in which the two drives competing within us can be, to take up Freud's terms 'fused' and 'de-fused'; and indeed *con*fused. It attests perhaps more potently than any other phenomenon of psychic life how obscure our desires are prone to become, how little we know of them. Driven by the unfathomably contradictory logic of the unconscious, they confound every intuition and reasonable expectation of the conscious mind.

Literature and cinema have, of course, proved rich resources for the exploration of the strange counter-rationality of masochism, from Leopold von Sacher-Masoch, de Sade and Georges Bataille to *Blue Velvet* and *Secretary*. But I want to edge towards a conclusion of this chapter and this book by, appropriately enough, invoking the cherished texts of my childhood. Following Freud himself, I detect some of the most compulsively destructive motifs concealed in the most 'innocent' childhood games, and especially in their repetition. The 'game' I have in mind is the famous ritual replayed forty-seven times in as many years in the course of Charles Schulz's *Peanuts* strip, in which Lucy lures Charlie Brown into running up to a football as she holds it in place at the tip, and kicking it. The outcome never changes: she pulls the ball away just as his foot is about to make contact, causing him to fly upwards and crash-land on his back. Lucy's lure is different each time, and each time overcomes the resistance accumulated by so much bitter experience: she accuses him of mistrusting women – 'Do you mistrust even your mother?'; she hands him a 'programme' officially scheduling the kick; she advises him to watch her eyes in order to gauge what she's going to do. And the last frame always sees her stand over him offering a few words of quietly sadistic explanation: 'I'm not your mother Charlie Brown'; 'In every programme, Charlie Brown, there are always a few last minute changes'; or simply, in the third case, donning a pair of dark glasses.

The enigmatic question the sequence raises, however, is not what drives Lucy's malevolent prank, but what drives her victim's compulsive repetition of the kick he knows (even as he's seduced into repressing his knowledge) he'll be denied. Why, in short, does Charlie Brown time after time charge headlong into his own trauma?

In fact, the invocation of the compulsion to repeat, though

irresistible, is also inadequate for explaining this particular repetition. As the *fort-da* game showed, repetition is motivated by the imperative to master trauma. Certainly, this is Charlie Brown's manifest intention, as his ritual intonation during his run-up of 'This year I'm gonna kick that ball clear over the moon' indicates. But I can't help feeling that this expression of phallic potency ('Poor old Charlie Brown', as his friends say – what's he done to deserve this reading?) disguises a more fundamental desire to *miss* the ball. In other words, his life-drive ('This year I'm gonna . . .') is unwittingly tethered to his death drive ('*WUMP*').

The theory of co-excitation, of the 'internal processes' which, especially when they surpass a certain threshold of intensity, induce 'a libidinal sympathetic excitation', offers one way into Charlie Brown's masochism. What cements the association here is Freud's inclusion of 'being thrown up in the air' in the repertory of infantile sexual stimuli. Is the round-headed kid impelled by the unconscious memory of a time when pain mysteriously begat pleasure?

No doubt this is taking things too far (but then again, there could be no psychoanalysis without taking things too far). The more basic point about Charlie Brown's masochistic charge (and this motif runs through other storylines: recall his abject failure to fly a kite, which repeats the same agonised sequence of furious running, momentary aerial suspension and violent crash-landing) is that it revives the infantile condition of helplessness: 'The masochist wants to be treated like a small and helpless child'.

But why should this be the case? What is concealed in this desire to be made helpless? The recent work of Jean Laplanche has done much to cast light on this question. Laplanche shows that it's the condition of helplessness that we first experience the touch of another (most obviously of our carers), that our body is first subjected to enigmatic and disturbing excitations. These touches or 'messages', emanating from a source the infant is unable to control or even identify, are simultaneously traumatic (an 'effraction or breaking in characteristic of *pain*'[11] writes Laplanche) *and* the means by which sexuality is inaugurated in us. In other words, *sexuality is originally masochistic*. To desire helplessness, vulnerability to a controlling and potentially destructive other, is to seek to return sexuality to its inaugural state.

Our inquiry into Freud began with Emma, whose trauma also revived the spectre of infantile helplessness. But Emma's response was very different from Charlie Brown's – it was aimed at containing her helplessness by localising it within a particular context (being in a shop alone). Emma is no masochist, in spite of her return to her grinning abuser. She returned in the (unconscious and impossible) hope that she might gain some understanding and control over the traumatic excitation he induced.

Beginning with hysteria, we discovered the peculiar *rationality* of unconscious defences. The hysteric is preserving herself from her own drive to self-destruction, from wanting what will harm her. The masochist, in contrast, affirms life not by defending against but by *embracing* his own helplessness, by charging recklessly towards the football that will time and again traumatize him. Masochism reveals the ultimate *irra*tionality of our desires.

The lateness of Freud's inquiries into masochism attests to the courage of his great enterprise, his willingness to expose it to phenomena which might undo its law-bound rationality. Masochism ends the pretence (much indulged by Freud and his orthodox disciples, it must be said) of psychoanalysis as the scientific anatomization and systematization of mental life, for it shows that mental life is precisely what refuses to conform to any system. But this failure of one kind of science is also the triumph of another, a science premised on the limits imposed by its object. Psychoanalysis is above all a way not of mastering but of living with the tormenting unknowability of my desires, and indeed, with my helplessness before them. Is this a pessimistic teaching? For the imperial scientific spirit, no doubt. But for the rest of us, it's as affirmative as it is disturbing. If we could know and satisfy our desires as animals do theirs, our lives would no doubt be easier. They'd also be a great deal less interesting, indeed, a great deal less worth living. Neither my words nor those of others would be worth the trouble if they weren't, as Freud has shown us, so tantalizingly difficult to read.

NOTES

1 Letter 69 of 'Extracts from the Fliess Papers' in *The Standard Edition of the Complete Psychological Works of Sigmund Freud*, Volume 1. Ed. James Strachey (Vintage, 2001), p. 259.

2 Because of the specific association of 'fantasy' in English with fanciful products of the imagination, I'm following the preference of British psychoanalytic writers for 'phantasy' as a translation of Freud's term *Phantasie* throughout this book (unless I want to convey the former meaning). Freud's term denotes an imaginary scene which plays out the fulfilment of an unconscious wish.

3 In fact, I am reading infantile sexuality into the Emma case retrospectively: Freud was yet to discover it at the time of writing the 'Project'.

4 The extract makes use of the technical abbreviations, specific to Freud's 'metapsychological' writings, '*Ucs.*', '*Pcs.*' and '*Cs.*'. These denote, respectively 'Unconscious', 'Preconscious' and 'Conscious'. The meaning of each term is explained.

5 Herman Melville, *The Confidence Man* (Penguin, 1991). Hereafter referred to as *CM*.

6 Hans Christian Andersen, 'The Emperor's New Clothes', in *Fairy Tales* (Everyman, 1992).

7 Paul Celan, 'Speak, You Also' in *Selected Poems*, trans. Michael Hamburger (Penguin, 1990).

8 Nathaniel Hawthorne, 'The Minister's Black Veil', in *Nathaniel Hawthorne: Tales* (Norton, 1986).

9 Adam Biro, *Two Jews on a Train*, trans. Catherine Tihanyi (University of Chicago Press, 2001).

10 Jacques Lacan, 'The Mirror Stage as Formative of the Function of

the I', in *Écrits: A Selection*, trans. Alan Sheridan (Routledge, 1989), p. 6.

11 Jean Laplance, 'Masochism and the General Theory of Seduction' in *Essays on Otherness* (Routledge, 1999), p. 209.

CHRONOLOGY

1856 6 May born in Freiberg, Moravia.

1860 Family moves to Vienna.

1873 Enters University as a medical student.

1876–82 Works under Ernst Brücke at Vienna Institute of Physiology.

1877 First publications on the anatomy of eels and sea lamprey.

1881 Graduates as MD.

1882 Engaged to Martha Bernays.

1882–5 Works at Vienna General Hospital.

1882 Learns from Josef Breuer of case of Anna O.

1884–7 Research into clinical uses of cocaine.

1885 Appointed *Privatdozent* (Lecturer) in Neuropathology.

1885–6 Studies under Charcot at the Salpêtrière in Paris. Interest turns to nervous diseases.

1886 Marriage to Martha Bernays. Sets up private practice for the treatment of nervous diseases.

1887 Introduces hypnosis into private practice. Birth of Martha, eldest of six children.

1887–1902 Friendship and correspondence with Wilhelm Fliess.

1889 Witnesses Hyppolite Bernheim's hypnotic experiments in Nancy.

1891 Monograph on aphasia

1893 Publishes 'Preliminary Communication' of clinical findings on hysteria with Breuer.

1893–8 Various short papers on hysteria, obsessions and anxiety.

1895 Publishes *Studies on Hysteria* with Breuer. Drafts *Project for a Scientific Psychology* – sent to Fliess incomplete, and published only posthumously in 1950.

1896 First use of term 'psychoanalysis'. Father dies, aged 80.

1897 Begins self-analysis. Abandonment of 'seduction theory' which rooted neurosis in actual experiences of sexual abuse, in favour of theory of infantile sexuality.

1900 *The Interpretation of Dreams.*

1901 *The Psychopathology of Everyday Life.*

1905 Publishes 'Dora' case; *Three Essays on The Theory of Sexuality*; *Jokes and Their Relation to the Unconscious.*

1906 Carl Gustav Jung, a Zurich Psychiatrist, becomes an adherent of psychoanalysis.

1908 First international meeting of psychoanalysts in Salzburg.

1909 Freud travels to USA with Jung, where he delivers the *Five Lectures on Psychoanalysis*. Case histories of 'Little Hans' and the 'Rat Man'.

1911 Alfred Adler, initially an adherent of Freud, forms first breakaway movement from psychoanalysis. Publishes analysis of memoirs of Judge Schreber, a German jurist who fell victim to psychotic illness.

1913 *Totem and Taboo.*

1914 Jung secedes from psychoanalytic movement to form his own.

1915 Writes twelve 'metapsychological' papers, of which only five survive.

1915–17 *Introductory Lectures on Psychoanalysis.*

1920 Death of second daughter, Sophie; *Beyond the Pleasure Principle.*

1921 *Group Psychology and the Analysis of the Ego.*

1923 *The Ego and the Id*; diagnosed with cancer.

1926 *Inhibitions, Symptoms and Anxiety*

1930 *Civilisation and Its Discontents*; mother dies, aged 95.

1933 Freud's books burned by newly-elected Nazi Party in Berlin.

1938 Nazis invade Austria, Freud flees with family to London; *An Outline of Psychoanalysis.*

1939 23 September dies in London.

SUGGESTIONS FOR FURTHER READING

BY FREUD

There can be few more comprehensive introductions to Freud's own thought than his own:

Introductory Lectures on Psychoanalysis (1915–17), Volumes 15–16 of the *Standard Edition* (Vintage, 2001)

New Introductory Lectures on Psychoanalysis (1932), Volume 22 of the *Standard Edition*

Two good readers with different and complementary emphases are:

Anna Freud (ed.), *Sigmund Freud: The Essentials of Psychoanalysis* (Penguin, 1986)

Peter Gay (ed.), *The Freud Reader* (Vintage, 1995)

FREUD'S LIFE

Ernest Jones, *The Life and Work of Freud* (Basic Books, 1993). Abridged version of Jones's 3-Volume life, completed in 1957.

Peter Gay, *Freud: A Life of Our Times* (Norton, 1998)

GENERAL OVERVIEWS

Richard Wollheim, *Freud* (Fontana, 1991)

Janet Malcolm, *Psychoanalysis: The Impossible Profession* (Granta, 2004). Both an incisive introduction to Freud and a gripping portrait of a practicing analyst.

Stephen Frosh, *For and Against Psychoanalysis* (Routledge, 1997)

Jean Laplanche and Jean-Bertrand Pontalis, *The Language of Psychoanalysis* (Karnac, 1988)

PSYCHOANALYSIS AFTER FREUD
1. *'Orthodox' Freudians*
Anna Freud, *The Ego and Its Mechanisms of Defence* (Karnac, 1992). A classic of ego-psychology from 1936.
Otto Fenichel, *The Psychoanalytic Theory of Neurosis* (Norton, 1995)

2. *Melanie Klein*
Juliet Mitchell (ed.), *The Selected Melanie Klein*. With an excellent Editor's Introduction.
Melanie Klein, *Narrative of a Child Analysis* (Vintage, 1998)

3. *The 'Object-Relations' School*
Wilfred Bion, *Learning From Experience* (Karnac, 1984)
D. W. Winnicott, *Playing and Reality* (Routledge, 1989)

4. *Lacan*
Jacques Lacan, *The Four Fundamental Concepts of Psychoanalysis* (Norton, 1981). The best way into Lacan's notoriously dense thought and writing.
Malcolm Bowie, *Lacan* (Fontana, 1991)

5. *Contemporary Psychoanalysis*
Donald Meltzer, *Sincerity and Other Works* (Karnac, 1994). Collected Papers of a leading Kleinian.
Christopher Bollas, *The Shadow of the Object* (Free Association, 1987). A key text in contemporary object-relations theory.
Jean Laplanche, *Essays on Otherness*, ed. John Fletcher (Routledge, 1999). A leading thinker in the post-Lacanian tradition
André Green, *On Private Madness* (Karnac, 1996). Uniquely bridges British and French traditions.

APPLYING FREUD

Paul Ricoeur, *Freud and Philosophy* (Yale, 1977)

Leo Bersani, *The Freudian Body: Psychoanalysis, Philosophy and Art* (Columbia, 1990)

Adam Phillips, *Darwin's Worms* (Faber, 1999)

Juliet Mitchell, *Psychoanalysis and Feminism* (Penguin, 1990)

Sander L. Gilman, *Freud, Race and Gender* (Princeton, 1993)

WEB RESOURCES

http://www.freud.org.uk/ Website of the London Freud Museum

http://www.aihp-iahp.com/ Website of the International Association for the History of Psychoanalysis

http://www.loc.gov/exhibits/freud/ Website for the Library of Congress' 1999 exhibition, Freud: Conflict and Culture

INDEX